Regulating Consumer Product Safety

EVALUATIVE STUDIES OF
HEALTH, SAFETY, AND ENVIRONMENTAL PROGRAMS

Marvin H. Kosters, Director
Center for the Study of Government Regulation
The American Enterprise Institute for Public Policy Research

Nuclear Safety: Risks and Regulation
William C. Wood

Regulating Consumer Product Safety
W. Kip Viscusi

The Regulation of Air Pollutant Emissions from Motor Vehicles
Lawrence J. White

The Regulation of Pharmaceuticals: Balancing the Benefits and Risks
Henry G. Grabowski and John M. Vernon

Regulating Consumer Product Safety

W. Kip Viscusi

American Enterprise Institute for Public Policy Research
Washington and London

W. Kip Viscusi is professor of business administration and director of the Center for Study of Business Regulation, Fuqua School of Business, Duke University.

Library of Congress Cataloging in Publication Data

Viscusi, W. Kip.
  Regulating consumer product safety.

  (AEI studies ; 400)
  Bibliography: p.
  1. Product safety—Law and legislation—United
States. I. Title. II. Series.
KF3945.V57 1984   344.73'042   84-2865
ISBN 0-8447-3548-5   347.30442
ISBN 0-8447-3547-7 (pbk.)

1 3 5 7 9 10 8 6 4 2

AEI Studies 400

©1984 by the American Enterprise Institute for Public Policy Research, Washington, D.C., and London. All rights reserved. No part of this publication may be used or reproduced in any manner whatsoever without permission in writing from the American Enterprise Institute except in the case of brief quotations embodied in news articles, critical articles, or reviews. The views expressed in the publications of the American Enterprise Institute are those of the authors and do not necessarily reflect the views of the staff, advisory panels, officers, or trustees of AEI.

"American Enterprise Institute" and   are registered service marks of the American Enterprise Institute for Public Policy Research.

Printed in the United States of America

850818

LIBRARY
ALMA COLLEGE
ALMA, MICHIGAN

Contents

PREFACE ix

1 WHY REGULATE PRODUCT SAFETY? 1

Are Markets Adequate? 2
Product Risk Insurance 7
Product Liability 8

2 MODES OF INTERVENTION 19

Policy Options 20
Valuing Risk Reduction 26
The Agenda for Policy 30

3 THE REGULATORY STRATEGY OF THE CPSC 33

Overview of the CPSC 33
Policy Options 41
Enforcement Mechanisms 46
Product Hazard Information 48
Conclusion 55

4 AN OVERVIEW OF CPSC POLICIES 57

Imminent Hazard Actions, Recalls, and Corrective
Actions 61
Voluntary Standards 64
General Characteristics of CPSC Policies 65
The Problem of Regulatory Uncertainty 67

5 THE EFFECT ON PRODUCT SAFETY 71

Accident Trends 71
The Mattress Flammability Standard 73
Child-resistant Bottle Caps 76
Crib Regulations 80
Swimming Pool Slides, Carpets and Rugs, and
Bicycles 82
Conclusion 85

6 BENEFITS AND COSTS OF CPSC REGULATIONS   88

The Matchbook Standard   89
The Architectural Glazing Standard   92
The Power Lawn Mower Standard   93
Unvented Gas-fired Space Heaters   96
Urea Formaldehyde Foam Insulation   99
Conclusion   101

7 POLICY PROPOSALS   106

BIBLIOGRAPHY   113

LIST OF TABLES

1. Product Liability Cases, 1974–1982   9
2. Distribution of Product Liability Awards for Large-Loss Claims, 1979   12
3. Payments and Losses in Bodily Injury Cases, by Economic Loss Range, 1976   13
4. Distribution of Payments in Bodily Injury Cases, by Severity of Injury, 1976   14
5. Distribution of Payments in Bodily Injury Cases, by Injury Diagnosis, 1976   15
6. Summary of Principal Studies of Dollar-Risk Trade-offs   28
7. Accidental Death Rates and Distribution of Accidents by Type, 1981   34
8. Distribution of Accidental Deaths by Cause, 1981   35
9. The Ten Products Involved in the Most Injuries, 1981   36
10. Budget and Staff of Major Risk-Regulation Agencies, 1982   38
11. CPSC Budget and Staff, Fiscal Years 1973–1982   40
12. CPSC Compliance Activities, Fiscal Year 1982   47
13. NEISS Data on Extension Ladder Injuries, 1974–1981   51
14. Injuries Associated with Recreational Activities, 1981   53
15. Injuries Associated with Recreational Equipment, 1981   54
16. Summary of CPSC Standards   58

17. Summary of CPSC Bans 59
18. Summary of CPSC Informational Requirements 59
19. Home Accidents, 1960–1981 72
20. Fire-related Deaths, 1960–1981 75
21. Poisonings, 1968–1981 77
22. Crib Injuries, 1973–1981 81
23. Injuries from Swimming Pool Slides and from
    Carpets and Rugs, 1974–1981 83
24. Bicycle Injuries, 1974–1981 84

The American Enterprise Institute for Public Policy Research, established in 1943, is a nonpartisan research and educational organization supported by foundations, corporations, and the public at large. Its purpose is to assist policy makers, scholars, businessmen, the press, and the public by providing objective analysis of national and international issues. Views expressed in the institute's publications are those of the authors and do not necessarily reflect the views of the staff, advisory panels, officers, or trustees of AEI.

Council of Academic Advisers

Paul W. McCracken, *Chairman, Edmund Ezra Day University Professor of Business Administration, University of Michigan*

*Kenneth W. Dam, *Harold J. and Marion F. Green Professor of Law, University of Chicago*

Donald C. Hellmann, *Professor of Political Science and International Studies, University of Washington*

D. Gale Johnson, *Eliakim Hastings Moore Distinguished Service Professor of Economics and Chairman, Department of Economics, University of Chicago*

Robert A. Nisbet, *Adjunct Scholar, American Enterprise Institute*

Herbert Stein, *A. Willis Robertson Professor of Economics, University of Virginia*

James Q. Wilson, *Henry Lee Shattuck Professor of Government, Harvard University*

*On leave for government service.

Executive Committee

Richard B. Madden, *Chairman of the Board*

William J. Baroody, Jr., *President*

James G. Affleck

Willard C. Butcher

Paul F. Oreffice

Richard D. Wood

Tait Trussell,
Vice President, Administration

Joseph J. Brady,
Vice President, Development

Edward Styles, *Director of Publications*

Program Directors

Russell Chapin, *Legislative Analyses*

Denis P. Doyle, *Education Policy Studies*

Marvin Esch, *Seminars and Programs*

Thomas F. Johnson, *Economic Policy Studies*

Marvin H. Kosters,
Government Regulation Studies

Jack A. Meyer, *Health Policy Studies*

Howard R. Penniman/Austin Ranney,
Political and Social Processes

Robert J. Pranger, *International Programs*

Periodicals

AEI Economist, Herbert Stein,
Editor

AEI Foreign Policy and Defense Review,
Evron M. Kirkpatrick, Robert J.
Pranger, and Harold H. Saunders,
Editors

Public Opinion, Seymour Martin
Lipset and Ben J. Wattenberg,
Co-Editors; Everett Carll Ladd,
Senior Editor; Karlyn H. Keene,
Managing Editor

Regulation, Anne Brunsdale,
Managing Editor

Preface

The emergence in the 1970s of a large number of government agencies focusing on risk regulation has led to considerable interest among economists in the merits of such regulation. Research on this issue has addressed not only broad principles for risk regulation but also the effectiveness of particular agencies' policies. Compared with other risk regulation agencies, the Consumer Product Safety Commission has been the focus of very little outside analysis and evaluation. Although this lack of attention may be attributable in part to the comparatively small budget of the agency, the broad scope of its mandate and its potential significance for product safety make it a fruitful target for analysis.

This monograph is an effort to analyze the design of the CPSC's strategy, its effectiveness, and profitable ways in which its policies can be redirected. Because there were comparatively few studies of the agency in the literature, I do not so much synthesize research findings as attempt to provide a comprehensive policy analysis of the commission's activities. In analyzing the desirability of these efforts, I apply a wide variety of principles for risk regulation that have been developed in other contexts but are nevertheless applicable. The literature on the value of life and on the appropriate way for society to approach the risk-dollar trade-offs that inevitably arise in regulating risks, for example, plays a fundamental role here as in studies of other risk regulation agencies.

In addition to providing a critique of the overall regulatory strategy, I review data on product safety trends to assess the effects of the CPSC's efforts and their overall merits. In this statistical analysis, I sacrifice depth for breadth. Although I am undertaking a refined study of some specific issues that arose under a concurrent National Science Foundation research grant, the analysis presented here is not so narrowly focused.

The reason for my emphasis on a broad policy perspective is that the most fundamental shortcomings of the CPSC do not hinge on any particularly new economic hypotheses that need to be tested or refined. The basic shortcoming, which is shared by most other risk regulation agencies, is that there is little concern about the overall economic desirability of the regulation. Discussions of shortcomings of the safety levels provided through market outcomes do not play a prominent role in CPSC decisions, nor does the CPSC adequately recognize the importance of making trade-offs between the costs of compliance and the risks that will be reduced. Besides these familiar problems, the CPSC has some distinctive deficiencies that distinguish it from other risk regulation agencies. The most prominent of these is that the legal authority of the CPSC enables it to sidestep the rule-making process that is required for new regulations and instead to concentrate its activities on ad hoc ban and recall actions that are not subject to the checks embodied in the rule-making procedure.

I presented the initial findings of the study at an American Enterprise Institute Conference on Health, Safety, and the Environment in 1981. At that conference I benefited from the comments of three discussants: Walter Oi, Sharon Oster, and Susan King. Many other individuals have provided useful suggestions since that time. Most important among these was Marvin Kosters, who made line-by-line comments on two drafts and helped to stimulate my initial interest in this topic. Finally, I would particularly like to thank Philip Harter, whose contribution to my treatment of product liability law made that section much sounder than it would otherwise have been.

1
Why Regulate Product Safety?

The Consumer Product Safety Commission (CPSC) estimates that each year "36 million Americans are injured and 30,000 are killed in accidents involving consumer products."[1] Although such statistics are cited by the CPSC as a justification for more stringent regulations, they actually tell us very little about the need for regulation. Even when a product is involved in an accident, the responsibility for the accident is usually shared by the person who suffers it. Sofa flammability, for example, is related to safety primarily for smokers and their families, who may also be victims of fires. More fundamentally, even if a product contributes to an accident, regulation may not be warranted because it will not usually be desirable to ensure that all products pose the lowest possible risk.

A more appropriate procedure than the excessive emphasis on risks that characterizes the CPSC's strategy is to assess the inadequacies of market processes and how they might be improved. In the absence of market failure, the government should not intervene. The economic processes that affect product safety outcomes have conceptual elements similar to those of market transactions involving other risks. As a consequence, there are many economic parallels between consumers' purchases of risky products, workers' decisions to be employed at hazardous firms, automobile owners' purchase of smaller and more hazard-prone cars, and homeowners' decisions to live in polluted sections of town.

With an adequately functioning market, the price or wage will adjust to reflect the relative risk and individuals' valuation of it. Even if consumers cannot assess product safety risks with pinpoint accuracy, products perceived as hazardous are nevertheless affected. Consumers will select a more hazardous product only if some additional characteristic, such as a lower price, offers an offsetting advantage. Sometimes the advantage is nonmonetary; people go bowling because of the pleasure the sport affords them even though 19,000 people annually are injured in it.

Since prices are measurable in well-ordered, quantifiable units, it is often convenient to focus on price differences for products of differing riskiness, holding other product characteristics constant. This approach dates back to Adam Smith's analysis of labor market risks, in which he argued that workers must receive higher wages if they are to be induced to accept risky jobs.[2] The existence of wage premiums for risk has been documented in a number of studies during the past decade.[3] The parallel with product safety is quite direct, since safer products command higher prices.[4]

With smoothly functioning markets, decentralized decisions by individuals and firms will lead to efficient levels of risk. If the benefits from improved safety exceed the costs of additional risk reduction, the market will generate safer products until no such discrepancy remains. Perhaps the most attractive feature of market outcomes is that they can promote efficient risk levels without any centralized calculation of the merits of different alternatives or any form of regulatory intervention.

There are two principal implications for observable market outcomes. First, the efficient level of risk will typically not be zero. Since improving product safety will generally entail additional costs, the optimal degree of safety hinges on the amount of those costs and the incremental benefits to consumers of further improvements.

Second, the safety of a product, like its other characteristics, is valued differently by different consumers. Since safety is a normal characteristic of products, wealthier consumers will tend to purchase safer goods.[5] This effect arises wholly apart from the effect of educational differences on ability to identify the risks posed by products. Because of the heterogeneity in risk-dollar trade-offs induced by differences in wealth and other factors, uniform product quality will not be optimal. A fundamental advantage of market-provided products is that the diversity of safety levels enables consumers to select the product most appropriate for their own preferences—preferences not only with respect to risk but also with respect to such features as size and ease of use. In contrast, government-mandated uniformity of product characteristics sacrifices the benefits that derive from diversity.

Are Markets Adequate?

If product markets functioned smoothly, there would be no basis for government intervention, and one could readily dismiss all such intrusions in the marketplace. The linchpin of the perfectly functioning market is that consumers and producers be fully cognizant of the risks their choices entail. This assumption clashes with the widespread belief that consumers do not have accurate information about product risks. Although there may be a similar lack of knowledge about other product characteristics, such as the likely taste of a new cereal, there are no large losses associated with mistaken choices of such characteristics.

Unfortunately, the evidence on the accuracy of consumers' perceptions of risk does not fully resolve the issue of whether risk perceptions are accurate. Although workers' risk perceptions are strongly correlated with their industrywide injury rates, there is no comparable evidence to suggest that consumers' risk assessments follow reasonable patterns.[6] The most that has ever been shown is that risk perceptions follow a generally plausible pattern; the extent of any discrepancy between actual and perceived risks has not been ascertained.

A phenomenon that might be viewed as evidence of consumer misperceptions is the large number of complaints by consumers to the CPSC and other consumer-oriented groups.[7] Although mistaken product choices may lead to complaints, the existence of even large numbers of complaints does not imply that consumer perceptions of product quality are inaccurate.

Consider a compact car that poses a known 1/1,000 greater chance of serious injury in an accident but remains an attractive purchase because of its greater fuel efficiency and lower price. Although the car may be a desirable purchase even though it poses a known risk, the small fraction of the users who actually suffer motor vehicle injuries will probably be dissatisfied. The difficulty is that we cannot readily distinguish whether their complaints are due to misperceived product safety risks or simply to dissatisfaction with the unfavorable outcome of lotteries entailing known risks. If the latter influence is dominant, consumer complaints provide no evidence of market failure.

Some experimental evidence indicates that people systematically underestimate low probabilities of adverse outcomes.[8] Whether these results pertain more broadly to choices where the individual has a substantial interest in the outcome is unclear. Evidence from the labor market suggests that there is a very strong correlation between workers' risk perceptions and their industries' injury and illness rates. Although this evidence does not imply that workers have perfect information, it does indicate a systematic component of market behavior along the lines assumed for well-functioning markets.

Systematic responses do not, however, imply that risk perceptions are completely accurate. In a study of purchases of flood insurance, Kunreuther found that many homeowners did not purchase heavily subsidized flood insurance even though they lived in flood-

3

prone areas.[9] Their decisions may reflect irrational behavior, or they may be made simply because the transactions costs of obtaining flood insurance outweigh the benefits of the government subsidy. Since uncertainty complicates consumers' choices, the possible difficulties created by imperfect information for how individuals assess risks and how they make choices are substantial, as emphasized by Arrow.[10]

While recognizing a potentially productive role for government policy, we should not lose sight of the productive aspects of the market system. Consumers need not make safety-related decisions on sheer whim. They can use a variety of sources of information in making their risk judgments—inspection of the product, the reputation of the producing firm, the provision of guarantees, and their own past experience and that of other consumers of the product. A consumer's own experience with a commodity is an important source of information when he uses it repeatedly and must decide whether to purchase the same or a different brand. Learning by experience may take the form of observing whether the product causes an injury. Less costly forms of learning include observing the performance of characteristics of a product that influence the chance of injury—for example, noticing that a set of bicycle brakes does not perform well. Much of the learning may be about how one should use the product. Knives, for example, are potentially dangerous, but the need for care is apparent. Thus far there has been no government effort to have all knives labeled with "caution" signs.

In many situations in which government intervention is considered, individual experimentation plays a central role in altering consumers' perceptions and their safety-related actions. Consumers can then alter their use of the products and their future purchasing patterns. Workers who quit their jobs because of job risks account for one-third of all quitting, and a similar learning effect may be important for product risks as well.[11] Just as workers quit hazardous jobs, consumers will stop using products as they learn about the hazards posed. This learning may, however, be costly since the event that conveys information may be a product-related injury.

More fundamentally, in situations in which such learning occurs, consumers will find experimentation with products whose implications are not fully understood to be relatively attractive in repeat purchase situations, where they can repeat the purchase of a product found to be safe and cease using a product found to be risky. Consumers often experiment with products with qualities that are uncertain, such as new brands of margarine.

Ideally, consumers would like to avoid the costs in injuries and mistaken purchases that are associated with this learning process.

4

Since better information about product risks would clearly be valued by consumers, we would expect that a market mechanism would supply it fully. To the extent that commercial ratings (such as those by Underwriters' Laboratories and *Consumer Reports*) are limited in scope, we might conclude that provision of further information would not be worth the cost. The deviant properties of information as an economic commodity, however, undermine any such conclusion.[12]

The first differentiating characteristic of information is its nonexcludability. A firm cannot easily limit information to those who are willing to pay for it; if it attempts to charge for safety information through a higher price, only the purchasers of the good will bear the cost. Those who make use of the information about the hazards associated with a product by avoiding its purchase make no contribution to the cost of providing the information.

Second, will this product safety information be credible? What incentives do firms have to give consumers accurate information about their products, and under what circumstances will consumers believe firms' product ratings? A running-shoe company might claim that its more expensive shoes are more likely to prevent injuries; should this claim be believed, or is it simply a way to reap a higher price for its shoes? The recent economic literature on information suggests that such rating systems will be credible only if the cost of certifying that the product is safe increases for more risky products, as it would if the product was sold with a warranty.[13]

A third class of difficulties stems from the interdependence of firms in an industry. In much the same way that low-quality used cars lead consumers to believe that used cars tend to be "lemons," injuries related to particular groups of products may lead consumers to assess entire categories of products as inherently risky. If a firm grades the relative safety of its products, will buyers believe that the ratings are applicable industrywide? To the extent that consumers judge products as a group (as the CPSC injury surveillance data system does) and not as the products of a specific firm, the enterprise will be conferring a benefit on the rest of the industry for which the firm receives no compensation whenever it advertises safety improvements or changes its products so as to improve the industrywide performance of the particular good.

Finally, it is often unclear whether advertising that improvements in safety have been made will raise or lower consumers' perceptions of risk. After major recalls of defective products, firms did not advertise that Ford Pintos' gas tanks were less likely to explode or that Mr. Coffee coffeemakers no longer posed fire hazards. Moreover, to the extent that individuals display a preference for learning about products through direct experimentation, there will be an incentive not to interfere with this process. Particularly alarming risks, such as the tampering with Tylenol capsules that led to seven deaths by poison, may lead to total depression of the demand for the product. In this case, Johnson and Johnson lost 87 percent of its Tylenol sales. In such extreme cases, advertisements certifying that the earlier risk had been eliminated would do little to dampen sales and might be the only possible means of recapturing the product's former market position.

Although market mechanisms alone cannot be relied on to provide the facts needed to make informed decisions, we do not now know whether risk assessments are systematically wrong or, if they are, in what direction and to what extent. We can, however, draw some broad distinctions. Readily perceived risks, such as most safety hazards, should pose little problem. Market processes work most effectively when consumers are informed of the risks, as they are in this case. In contrast, dimly understood health risks may be a matter of serious policy concern. These risks frequently arise from toxic substances that pose low probabilities of an illness with a deferred effect, often a decade or more after the initial exposure. The limitations of individual decision making appear to be greatest when dealing with very rare events and with effects that occur after a substantial lag. Health hazards are also, however, most susceptible to overregulation since the wide publicity devoted to newly discovered risks is frequently unduly alarmist and usually does not distinguish the degree of risk.

Before deciding whether to intervene in a particular situation, one should assess the information available to consumers and the degree to which any inadequacies in it merit serious concern. In the absence of more definitive general studies of information about product risks, this case-by-case approach appears to be the most promising.

There may be other rationales for government intervention, but their relative importance is less apparent. Society at large may have an altruistic interest in individuals' well-being, but whether that interest is significant when compared with the individual's own valuation of life and health is unclear. Another potential shortcoming is that there may be insufficient product differentiation in the market to meet the preferences of all specialized tastes. Although there is a strong conceptual literature on the possible inadequacies of the market-provided product mixture, the empirical importance of the effects has not been established.[14] Even if they are significant, the implications for product safety policies are unclear if one is considering regulations that will diminish the extent of product differentiation rather than increase it.

6

Product Risk Insurance

The risks posed by consumer products would have less adverse effect on individual welfare if consumers could be insured against all possible losses. Guarantees and warranties insure against damage to the product but not against harm to individuals. Private insurance companies do not insure individual product risks but offer more comprehensive coverage for health and life. Although it is generally desirable to insure one's entire portfolio of risks rather than to insure individual risks separately, comprehensive insurance premiums do not vary according to consumer purchases (except for smokers) and consequently do not provide additional incentives for the selection of safer products.

Two fundamental drawbacks of compensation systems, such as insurance, appear to be important. First, although accident victims are awarded compensation, it may not restore their previous welfare. If the product has led to someone's death or serious permanent injury, no financial compensation could restore his previous welfare; nor would it be efficient for compensation to be that great.[15] Since life and health are nontransferable commodities, attempts to compensate accident victims will always be only partially effective.

The second shortcoming of these mechanisms is that compensation should depend on consumers' safety-related actions, which are difficult to monitor but often have a critical influence on the chance of an accident or an adverse effect on health. Was the consumer actually using a particular product? If so, was he doing so prudently? The importance of the degree of care is clear for safety hazards, such as those faced when riding a bicycle. The degree of care may be less apparent but equally important for health hazards. A particularly prominent case in which individual actions are important is with respect to the risks posed by asbestos in hair dryers, which increase dramatically for smokers.

Time lags pose additional problems since the effectiveness of insurance compensation is reduced in a world in which the causes of accidents cannot be determined readily. Responsibility for effects on health is often difficult to assign, particularly for health hazards that result in adverse outcomes, such as cancer, with a gestation period of a decade or more. The costs associated with determining responsibility in these cases may also have prevented the emergence of a more comprehensive system of product accident insurance. If companies must incur substantial legal fees to control misrepresentations of insurance claims, their incentive to offer insurance will be reduced.

Firms could, of course, offer no-fault coverage. Its costs would be substantial, both because consumers tend to exercise less care if they are insured and because the less cautious consumers would gravitate toward such insured products. If a manufacturer of skis offered $25,000 compensation to all those injured while wearing a particular model of skis, novices and those who wished to risk trying a challenging course that exceeded their abilities would buy the product. If only one-tenth of all users suffered broken legs, the cost of the skis would need to be $2,500 to cover the insurance alone. If the firm had a loss ratio of 50 percent to reflect the administrative costs associated with insurance, the price would be driven up to over $5,000. The insured skis would then be attractive only to an extremely high-risk group, which would exacerbate the adverse selection problem.

Finally, insurance and warranties are effective only if the firm has the funds to make the payments. Self-insured firms may find that filing for bankruptcy is more attractive than paying off a substantial set of insurance claims if an entire product line causes serious injury. It is for this reason that workers' compensation systems permit only relatively large firms to be self-insured.

Product Liability

The extent to which the market ensures optimal product safety depends in part on the legal and institutional context in which the market functions. The product liability system, through the responsibilities it places on producers, provides incentives for them to devote resources to improving safety. The primary legal responsibility for product safety is borne by the manufacturer, but to obtain financial compensation the injured consumer must bear the burden of initiating and carrying out the legal actions necessary to establish and adjudicate his claim for compensation.

Product liability lawsuits can be aptly characterized as a growth industry. Over the past decade, there has been a dramatic escalation in the number of product liability lawsuits, in part because of the development of strict liability criteria and their effects on the prospects of filing a successful case. The number of product liability cases filed in U.S. district courts rose by a factor of almost six from 1974 to 1982 (see table 1). This increase is not attributable solely to the increased litigiousness of society; the product liability share of all civil filings tripled during that period. The increase in product liability cases has led to efforts to establish a federal product liability law that would establish more uniform and weaker requirements than some state laws. Legal remedies for product safety problems are no longer a minor part of the process generating product safety, since firms are

must be "unreasonable"—the user appreciated the risk and did not exercise prudent judgment in incurring it[19]—before the plaintiff is barred from recovery. Like contributory negligence, assumption of the risk is an all-or-nothing legal position—the plaintiff either did or did not assume the risk. As a result, many states have enacted statutes that apportion responsibility for an injury among the various parties that contributed to it. It might be held, for example, that the manufacturer is two-thirds responsible for producing the unreasonably dangerous product but the injured person is one-third responsible for not being more careful. In that case, the plaintiff would recover two-thirds of the total damages.

Regardless of the liability concept, the consumer must establish that he was injured by the product. This link is particularly difficult to prove for chronic diseases such as cancer, which have multiple causes and long gestation periods before the illness becomes apparent. If a consumer has lung cancer, which, if any, asbestos-containing products played a contributory role? (For these ailments the statute of limitations in some states may long since have expired. As a result, there have been proposals to make the statute of limitations apply from the date of the illness's discovery instead of the date of exposure.) Even for many safety risks, it may be difficult to prove the link. The second requirement is to show that the injury occurred because the product was defective or unreasonably dangerous when it was produced.

If the consumer is successful in his case, he will receive an award to compensate him for damages. Punitive damage awards are possible, but they do not account for a major share of large awards. Less than 1 percent of awards in large liability claims, for example those greater than $100,000, include punitive damages.[20] Plaintiffs are ordinarily compensated only for actual damages incurred, principally direct financial costs. In large liability claims, 84 percent of all awards constitute compensation for wage losses, and 13 percent constitute direct medical costs. Table 2 summarizes the distribution of these large product liability awards. The total of the awards exceeds the direct financial costs incurred by only 20 percent; so there is a close relation between consumers' actual losses and the financial compensation they receive.

A more comprehensive perspective on the relation between accident losses and awards in bodily injury cases is provided by Insurance Services Office data on closed product liability claims (see table 3).[21] Severe losses (more than $100,000) have a payment/loss ratio of 0.99, which closely parallels the relation in the Alliance of American Insurers data for large claims. Successful claims under this amount receive

TABLE 2
DISTRIBUTION OF PRODUCT LIABILITY AWARDS FOR LARGE-LOSS CLAIMS, 1979
(percent)

Amount (dollars)	Bodily Injury Only		Property Damage Only		All Incidents	
	Incidents	$ claims	Incidents	$ claims	Incidents	$ claims
0	0.0	0.0	3.0	0.0	0.6	0.0
1–99,999	5.1	1.3	12.1	2.5	6.3	1.5
100,000–199,999	42.0	18.1	33.3	10.8	39.7	16.0
200,000–499,999	32.6	28.8	24.2	17.9	31.0	26.1
500,000–999,999	15.2	32.0	21.2	34.9	16.7	32.5
1,000,000 or more	5.1	19.8	6.1	33.9	5.7	24.0

NOTE: Percentages do not add to 100.0 because of rounding.

SOURCE: Alliance of American Insurers, "Highlights of Large-Loss Product Liability Claims" (1980), table 20.

TABLE 3

PAYMENTS AND LOSSES IN BODILY INJURY CASES, BY ECONOMIC LOSS RANGE, 1976

Economic Loss (dollars)	Number of Injured Parties	Average Payment (dollars)	Average Economic Loss (dollars)	Payment/Loss Ratio
0	798	1,766	0	NA
1–1,000	4,529	1,676	195	8.595
1,001–2,000	349	15,956	1,441	11.073
2,001–3,000	216	18,743	2,473	7.579
3,001–4,000	165	22,720	3,513	6.467
4,001–5,000	90	23,996	4,462	5.378
5,001–7,500	154	41,999	6,094	6.892
7,501–10,000	121	66,980	8,712	7.688
10,001–15,000	123	62,337	12,471	4.999
15,001–20,000	63	106,346	17,257	6.162
20,001–25,000	47	92,027	22,573	4.077
25,001–50,000	107	142,093	34,979	4.062
50,001–100,000	64	393,895	66,431	5.929
100,001–200,000	54	500,324	144,787	3.456
200,001–300,000	30	261,102	244,530	1.068
300,001–400,000	19	578,722	346,738	1.669
400,001–500,000	18	485,175	449,676	1.079
500,001–750,000	13	308,635	581,349	0.531
750,001–1,000,000	9	846,661	862,662	0.981
1,000,001 or more	10	389,208	2,593,242	0.150
Total	6,979	24,129	12,561	1.921

NA = not applicable.

SOURCE: Insurance Services Office, *Product Liability Closed Claims Survey* (New York, 1977), table 5-7. All figures are in 1976 prices.

more than proportional compensation. These data are not adjusted, however, to reflect the role of inflation or discounting.

The size of the awards primarily reflects monetary losses rather than pain and suffering. Tables 4 and 5 summarize the payments for principal health categories. The average award for fatal accidents is $226,000, which is comparable to the present value of future earnings for the typical prime-age male. The larger payments for permanent total disability and cancer are not unexpected since medical expenses play a significant role in determining the size of the awards.

TABLE 4

DISTRIBUTION OF PAYMENTS IN BODILY INJURY CASES, BY SEVERITY OF INJURY, 1976

Severity of Injury	Parties Receiving Payments (percent)	Average Payment (dollars)	Share of Total Payments (percent)
Death	3.6	225,881	18.8
Permanent total disability	3.0	434,143	29.9
Permanent partial disability	2.3	267,305	14.2
Temporary total disability	23.0	28,144	15.0
No disability	68.2	14,039	22.2
Total	100.0	43,163	100.0
Unknown	—	71,953	—

NOTE: Percentages do not add to 100.0 because of rounding.

SOURCE: Insurance Services Office, *Closed Claims Survey*, table 22-1, p. 113. All figures are in 1982 prices.

Although such awards may be a reasonable means of compensation, the valuation of these outcomes for purposes of preventing accidents is much larger. The product liability system's lack of emphasis on pain, suffering, and related concerns is not a matter of trivial concern with minor effects on the appropriateness of compensation. Economic analysis of the implicit values that workers place on their lives, which is discussed in chapter 3, suggests that they implicitly value their lives by roughly an order of magnitude more than their future lifetime earnings. Earnings-based compensation consequently significantly undercompensates victims.[22]

If a consumer is injured in a minor way or if the chance of winning a lawsuit is small, a product liability lawsuit will not be financially attractive. Legal costs are often on the order of $30,000 for large liability claims; so the transactions costs are substantial. If the consumer is disabled and deprived of his primary source of income, the prospect of an expensive lawsuit may discourage even a legitimate claim, although many lawyers will act for injured workers for a contingent fee.

Finally, pervasive cases of defective products may raise a quite different problem in that the manufacturer may be unable to pay all the awards or may be able to reorganize under current bankruptcy laws. This problem has received considerable attention recently as the Manville Corporation has resorted to bankruptcy proceedings to escape the burdens imposed by asbestos-related claims.

14

TABLE 5

DISTRIBUTION OF PAYMENTS IN BODILY INJURY CASES, BY INJURY
DIAGNOSIS, 1976

Injury Diagnosis	Parties Receiving Payments (percent)	Average Payment (dollars)	Share of Total Payments (percent)
Amputation	2.6	192,080	11.2
Asphyxiation	1.0	118,638	2.6
Bruise-abrasion	3.8	8,781	0.8
Burn	7.6	133,936	23.5
Concussion	0.7	55,214	0.9
Dermatitis	2.1	2,496	0.1
Dislocation	0.3	54,604	0.4
Electrical shock	0.3	53.938	0.4
Fracture	16.7	35,948	13.7
Laceration	14.5	19,108	6.4
Poisoning	16.1	1,873	0.7
Strain-sprain	3.4	42,837	3.4
Disease, respiratory	0.6	101,356	1.3
Disease, cancer (including Hodgkin's disease and leukemia)	0.3	283,701	1.8
Disease, other	0.9	29,604	0.6
Paraplegia	0.1	543,354	1.5
Quadriplegia	0.1	859,104	2.6
Brain damage	0.8	607,719	10.5
Other	28.1	27,416	17.6
Total	100.0	43,656	100.0
Unknown	—	67,306	—

SOURCE: Insurance Services Office, *Closed Claims Survey*, table 25-1, p. 116. All figures are in 1982 prices.

The existence of this shortcoming of product liability and self-insurance schemes is not new. Nuclear power plants pose risks sufficiently widespread that any major catastrophe would create more financial obligations than could be borne. Similarly, small firms are not self-insured under workers' compensation because of the limits of their ability to bear the liability. The current liability system is not well suited to dealing with very large and pervasive risks in relation to the financial resources of a company. Firms with product liability insurance, however, are better able to meet these costs.

Product liability consequently can at best play a partial role in

15

promoting product safety. Although some features of the current product liability system may be consistent with economic efficiency, the system also has serious deficiencies. The principles for compensation are not ideal, and the legal costs are often prohibitive. Since causality is often difficult to determine, health risks may not be adequately covered. Very large risks, such as those creating claims greater than a company's resources, create additional problems since companies can escape liability for such disasters. Although these deficiencies can be mitigated in part by changes in legislation to alter the basis for determining compensation, many of the problems are inherent. Despite these shortcomings, the product liability system can play a constructive role in fostering safety in the marketplace. The legal and institutional mechanisms that promote product safety must be taken into account in analyzing the potential role for government regulation of product safety.

The existence of product safety hazards does not in itself provide a basis for intervention by the CPSC. If consumers are fully informed of the risks they face, market outcomes will be efficient. Even in the absence of full knowledge of the hazards, the legal remedies available to consumers through the product liability system will bolster the incentives firms have to produce safe products. Although neither of these mechanisms may be fully effective, they do provide a constructive force for safety. In addition, they define the context for CPSC intervention. Failure to take these forces into account may result in government regulations that displace particularly effective safety-enhancing mechanisms.

Notes

1. See U.S. Consumer Product Safety Commission, *Annual Report*, pt. 1 (Washington, D.C., 1981), p. 13.

2. See Adam Smith, *The Wealth of Nations* (New York: Modern Library, 1937).

3. For a survey of this literature, see Robert S. Smith, "Compensating Differentials and Public Policy: A Review," *Industrial and Labor Relations Review*, vol. 32 (1979), pp. 339–52; Martin Bailey, *Reducing Risks to Life: Measurement of the Benefits* (Washington, D.C.: American Enterprise Institute, 1980); and W. Kip Viscusi, *Risk by Choice: Regulating Health and Safety in the Workplace* (Cambridge, Mass.: Harvard University Press, 1983).

4. The most comprehensive recent analysis of product safety in the spirit of the neoclassical approach is Walter Oi, "The Economics of Product Safety," *Bell Journal of Economics*, vol. 4 (1973), pp. 3–28. Product safety regulation is discussed within the context of similar regulatory efforts by Paul MacAvoy, *The Regulated Industries and the Economy* (New York: Norton, 1979); Henry

Grabowski and John Vernon, "Consumer Product Safety Regulation," *American Economic Review*, vol. 67 (1978), pp. 284–89; and Nina Cornell, Roger Noll, and Barry Weingast, "Safety Regulation," H. Owen and C. Schultze, eds., *Setting National Priorities: The Next Ten Years* (Washington, D.C.: Brookings Institution, 1976), pp. 457–504.

5. See W. Kip Viscusi, *Employment Hazards: An Investigation of Market Performance* (Cambridge, Mass.: Harvard University Press, 1979), and *Risk by Choice*, for a detailed conceptual and empirical analysis of the relation between job risks and workers' wealth. The time series evidence presented in the more recent volume suggests that this relation can be generalized to other risks as well.

6. Viscusi, *Risk by Choice*.

7. Complaints by consumers are a principal determinant of CPSC product safety investigations. A detailed empirical analysis of the determinants of consumer complaints is provided by Sharon Oster, "The Determinants of Consumer Complaints," *Review of Economics and Statistics*, vol. 62 (1980), pp. 603–9.

8. This experimental evidence is discussed by Marc Alpert and Howard Raiffa, "A Progress Report on the Training of the Probability Assessors," unpublished manuscript, Harvard University (1969); R. J. Arnould and H. Grabowski, "Auto Safety Regulation: An Analysis of Market Failure," *Bell Journal of Economics*, vol. 12 (1981), pp. 27–48; and others.

9. H. Kunreuther et al., *Disaster Insurance Protection: Public Policy Lessons* (New York: John Wiley and Sons, 1978).

10. Kenneth Arrow, "Risk Perception in Psychology and Economics," *Economic Inquiry*, vol. 20 (1982), pp. 1–9.

11. A nontechnical discussion of my work on the relation between job hazards and quits can be found in Viscusi, *Risk by Choice*.

12. The classic, seminal work in this area is that of Kenneth Arrow, *Essays in the Theory of Risk-Bearing* (Chicago: Markham Publishers, 1971).

13. See Michael Spence, *Market Signaling* (Cambridge, Mass.: Harvard University Press, 1974).

14. See in particular Michael Spence, "Monopoly, Quality, and Regulation," *Bell Journal of Economics*, vol. 6 (1975), pp. 417–29.

15. The key assumption generating this result is that, for any given level of income, one's marginal utility of income and overall welfare level are reduced if one is in ill health or is dead. See Michael Spence, "Consumer Misperceptions, Product Failure, and Producer Liability," *Review of Economic Studies*, vol. 44 (1977), pp. 561–72, and Viscusi, *Employment Hazards*, for derivations of this result.

16. Some states impose liability for injuries resulting from a defect in a product whether or not it is "unreasonably dangerous."

17. Under certain conditions strict liability can lead to an efficient system of accident compensation. See Steven Shavell, "Strict Liability vs. Negligence," *Journal of Legal Studies*, vol. 9 (1980), pp. 1–25.

18. Comments to Section 402A, *Restatement* (Second) *Torts* (1965).

19. A court held, for example, that even though someone was told the

brakes on his car were dangerously defective, it was not unreasonable for him to continue to drive it, and hence he was not barred from recovery.

20. See Alliance of American Insurers, "Highlights of Large-Loss Product Liability Claims," 1980, p. i. Other data in this paragraph are also drawn from this study. These estimates exclude factors such as inflation and discounting and are therefore only rough approximations.

21. Insurance Services Office, *Product Liability Closed Claims Survey* (New York: Insurance Services Office, 1977).

22. Even this degree of compensation for large claims may overstate the average rate of compensation. The discrepancy arises because large claims are made up disproportionately of cases in which there is quite substantial compensation while the cases of less complete compensation are not captured in the sample.

2
Modes of Intervention

Designers of risk regulation policies typically proceed from an identification of some outcome that they view as undesirable to adoption of highly structured standards requiring that the defect be eliminated. Although this legalistic approach has the advantage of simplicity, it ignores the role of existing market machanisms that promote safety as well as the economic mechanisms by which policies exert their influence. Firms marketing unsafe products will improve the safety of their products if they have a financial incentive to do so. Market mechanisms transmit these incentives through prices; consumers will pay lower prices for products they perceive as hazardous than for similar safe products.

Government regulations can influence safety by altering firms' financial incentive to provide safe consumer products. Hazardous products could be identified, with the incentive coming through the price mechanism. Firms producing products found to cause accidents could be penalized in much the same way as workers' compensation costs provide job safety incentives. In an extreme case, a product's characteristics could be regulated directly, as in bans of unsafe products. Although most actions of the CPSC have relied on direct regulation, all these mechanisms can potentially promote safe product attributes.

The observed level of product safety is jointly influenced by consumers' behavior and product attributes. Even if the characteristics of a product are altered, there is no guarantee that the desired level of safety will be ensured since consumers must also select their safety-related actions. If consumers choose not to wear seatbelts, to leave childproof caps off bottles, or to ride CPSC- approved bicycles faster because of the implied assurance of lower risks, they may subvert the intent of the policy.

These actions are not necessarily irrational; nor are they mere conjecture. If exercising more care is more costly, a consumer will have an incentive to reduce his safety-enhancing actions when using intrinsically safer products.[1] The principal documentation of the effect

19

has been for automobile safety; Peltzman has attributed the failure of seatbelts to enhance safety significantly to the effect of this response by drivers. Although the magnitude of the response remains controversial, the existence of some adverse influence on drivers' behavior is not subject to serious question. Analogous responses by consumers to CPSC regulations are considered later in this volume.

The primary limitation of this behavior for policy is that consumers' responses will dissipate, and perhaps even reverse, the desired safety improvements. It may not be feasible to alter consumers' responses since they cannot be readily monitored, whereas product characteristics can.

Policies will usually focus on actions by the firm rather than on the behavior of the consumer because they are easier to monitor, not because they are necessarily more important. Even though we cannot monitor consumers' actions, their behavior should not be ignored when considering the optimal policy design.

Policy Options

In addition to the option of not intervening at all, the government has two broad policy options—it can arrange some kind of compensation scheme for accident victims, or it can attempt to lower the risk. These options are not mutually exclusive since the compensation scheme may alter the risk by affecting consumers' decisions or firms' behavior.

Despite the various parallels between workers' safety and product safety, there is no analogue of a workers' compensation system for product-related accidents. Although compensation systems have spread to other areas of risk regulation, as in the Superfund for environmental wastes, there has been no comparable attempt to adopt a compensation system for product accidents. Some toxic tort proposals do, however, constitute a possible movement in that direction.

If an accident compensation system is merit rated so that firms with a higher accident record are penalized for their adverse performance, it will not only provide funds to compensate accident victims but also produce additional incentives for safety. When there is no link between accident performance and insurance premiums, the compensation system in effect subsidizes hazardous behavior, with the result that consumers purchase more risky products than they otherwise would. The workers' compensation system is weakly merit rated, and the Superfund includes no merit rating—chemical firms are taxed irrespective of their performance. Proposals that would tax chemical wastes rather than chemical inputs would be preferable. Job accidents can be merit rated since the employer's identity is known, whereas the party responsible for disposing of toxic wastes is typically not.

The principal difficulty with a product-accident version of workers' compensation is that of monitoring. Two links are critical in the job safety case. Not only must the insurer be able to identify the employer of the injured worker, but the employer must have some ability to monitor and influence the behavior of its workers to prevent careless actions that might drive up its premiums. For consumer products and the many ways in which they can be used, the compensation scheme might serve largely as a means of rewarding careless behavior. Indeed, it is usually not feasible to monitor even whether the consumer was using a particular product at the time of the accident. If the consumer knowingly undertook unsafe actions on his own volition, we can infer that his expected welfare from hazardous behavior was greater than from safe behavior. There is little justification on the basis of consumers' welfare for providing additional compensation to those who are injured under these circumstances, and, to the extent that such rewards encourage unsafe actions, there may be a strong policy interest against compensation schemes.

It is also difficult to monitor the safety performance of a company's products. Even if the role of consumers' actions was inconsequential, a merit-rating scheme would still necessitate a tally of the number of injuries with products such as Lawn Boy lawn mowers. Since the use of consumer products is decentralized throughout the entire economy, whereas accidents to workers occur within the workplace, the task of monitoring accidents firm by firm is inordinately larger for products than for jobs. If we cannot monitor the safety performance of firms or consumers with much accuracy, it is difficult to establish any form of merit-rated funding. The compensation system would then need to be funded through a levy unrelated to product safety, as the Superfund is.

Compensation not linked to performance creates no safety incentives. Its only constructive function is that it compensates accident victims. If we exclude any favorable incentive from accident compensation, it is difficult to make a compelling argument that those who are injured using consumer products should be compensated differently from those who are injured but not in conjunction with a product, such as someone who slips down a flight of stairs. The existing, broader social insurance programs appear best suited to this task.

A related set of policies attempts to alleviate the product safety problem itself, rather than compensate victims of accidents. These policies, which may be directed at altering the actions of the consumer, the producer, or both, include provision of safety information, penalties for accidents, penalty systems related to product characteristics, and outright bans or design requirements.

Providing information to consumers is potentially the least obtrusive of these mechanisms. It would complement market forces and, to the extent that the information enabled consumers to make more accurate risk assessments, would push market outcomes closer to those that would prevail if markets worked efficiently. A principal difference between the informational approach and the usual alternative—design standards—is that standards often greatly diminish the heterogeneity of available product quality while information about quality need not diminish the variety of products. In view of the considerable heterogeneity in attitudes toward risk, the potential economic losses from restricting the choices available to consumers may be substantial.

A competing concern relates to fixed costs and economies of scale that may prevail in the production process. The unit cost of making safety improvements in a small number of products may be high. The fixed costs of redesigning products and restructuring the production process may be prohibitive if the market for the product is small. When spread over a larger number of consumers, the cost of the safety improvements may be much more moderate, making the price of safe products attractive to a broad variety of consumers. Since tastes of minority groups of consumers, such as those with very strong preferences for product safety, may not always be met inexpensively by the market-provided product mixture, safety regulations could, in principle, promote more desirable consumer options in this instance.[2] While one cannot rule out the potential attractiveness of design standards, for goods produced in large quantities the fixed costs associated with safety features should not be a major barrier to a diverse product mix.

Although it is simple to assert the clear-cut benefits of making consumers better informed, the informational strategy does not consist of a precise statement of the probabilities of accident for different products under differing conditions of use. One would not, for example, tell consumers that they had a 1/10,000 chance of a toe injury if they mowed a level lawn and a 15/10,000 chance of such an injury on a hilly lawn. Our knowledge of the determinants of accidents is seldom so precise, and it is doubtful whether information in this form would be reliably understood and acted on by consumers. Ideally, a system for transferring information should employ a consistent grading of the relative risk, an indication of the degree of care or any special actions that the user of the product should undertake, and the presence of any important synergistic effects, such as the link between smoking and the risk from asbestos exposure.

To be effective, information must alter consumers' beliefs in some way. The consumer must learn something new about the nature of the risk, the efficacy of preventive action, or the severity of the risk. Many government policies designated as information oriented are directed at exhortation rather than at providing knowledge consumers do not already possess. Advertisements proclaiming that seatbelts save lives should be expected to have little effect on behavior since they are not telling consumers something they do not already know. Similarly, the increasingly alarming warnings on cigarette packages may have little effect to the extent that smokers are already aware of the risks and are incurring them knowingly.

Although consumers' responses to these efforts have not been dramatic, policies that convey new knowledge have much greater potential. One study of the effects of chemical labeling indicates that workers who have received warnings related to their exposure to hazardous chemicals (such as TNT and asbestos) revise their risk perceptions in the expected fashion.[3] Moreover, the wage differentials they demand for the newly perceived risks and the number who quit their jobs in response follow the expected patterns. What is particularly noteworthy about these chemical labeling results is that the primary determinant of the workers' response is not the level of the risk implied by the warning but its informational content. Informational policies that convey new information convincingly have better prospects of success than efforts designed to reinforce existing knowledge.

Much information is already provided to consumers through market mechanisms. Many firms and industries have voluntarily adopted forms of quality certification, including guarantees, warranties, and industry codes. The voluntary decision to undertake such certification is an important contributor to the informational value associated with it; producers are more likely to provide guarantees for reliable products since the cost of a guarantee is negatively correlated with the product's reliability.[4] As a result, the consumer can infer from a voluntarily provided guarantee that the producer views the product as comparatively sound. Moreover, since officials within an industry are often better able to develop more meaningful quality ratings for their products, a more appropriate rating system may emerge on a voluntary basis.

If, however, these "voluntary" efforts are adopted at the urgings of the CPSC or some other governmental group so as to forestall regulation, the benefits of voluntarism will be diluted. Consumers will not be able to conclude, for example, that products with mandatory warranties are necessarily safer. It will, however, be reasonable to believe that products meeting industry safety standards are safer even if the safety standards are mandatory. Voluntary grading systems may also be adopted, however, for quite different reasons, for example, to exclude smaller firms from the market. It is important to ascertain whether the voluntary effort is intended simply to limit competition from firms making lower-quality products.

Voluntary industry-rating schemes also raise important comparability problems. Each rating system for a product type may be designed quite reasonably, but if it is difficult for the consumer to judge relative risk among products, the benefits of the grading system will be reduced. The CPSC may be playing an unwitting role in creating confusion about risks since it permits firms to advertise that they are in compliance with CPSC standards even though such compliance does not guarantee a particular risk level for all possible uses of the product; nor does such a claim indicate that the product is safer than substitute products that might be used for a similar purpose.

A more direct method of improving product safety is to penalize firms for the risks posed by their products, an approach that has economic properties similar to those of strict liability. While an accident tax is feasible for accidents that can be monitored, such as those in the workplace, penalties for product-related accidents share all the shortcomings of merit-rating systems.

An alternative to penalizing on the basis of risk outcomes is to assess penalties on the basis of product characteristics correlated with riskiness. To do this requires criteria for assessing penalties, usually product standards, and a penalty schedule for violations. The use of this strategy is by no means as restrictive as past efforts involving the standards-penalty approach might suggest. There is usually considerable scope in selecting the nature of the standards, their level, and the penalties associated with violations.

I focus here on three dimensions in which standards can vary—their general nature, their scope and level, and their applicability. The first is the nature of the standard itself. The principal distinction is whether the standard is a performance standard or a specification standard. Performance standards are linked primarily to the risk-related performance of the product, for example, requiring that sofa fabrics meet certain flammability tests. Under a specification standard, the precise characteristics that the product must meet are delineated—for example, the particular sofa fabrics that are acceptable. The principal benefits of performance standards are that firms can select the least costly way of promoting product safety and the regulation is directly linked to product safety, thus fostering incentives to reduce hazards.

In practice, the distinction between performance and specification standards has become blurred. Since more flexible performance-oriented standards have come to be more favorably regarded, it has become rare for regulatory agencies not to characterize their regulations as performance oriented. In extreme instances, there may be only one feasible means of achieving a level of performance adequate for compliance, so that a performance standard becomes tantamount to a specification standard.

The second characteristic of a standard is the level at which it is set, in particular, the number of product characteristics subject to the regulation and the minimal levels that these characteristics must attain. Banning or recalling a product can be viewed as adopting a standard with an extreme scope.

It should be noted that standards need not entail a single cutoff point for compliance. One might, for example, impose high penalties for characteristics below level C_1, moderate penalties for characteristics between C_1 and C_2, and no penalties for characteristics above C_2, where C_1 is below C_2. In the limiting case of such distinctions, there could be continually increasing penalties as the value of the regulated product characteristic declined.

Such differentiation is an application of the more basic principle that the level and scope of the standard should ideally be set to maximize the net benefits to society. The incremental benefits from further tightening or broadening of the standard should equal the incremental costs at their optimal level. Although this benefit-cost criterion should not be particularly controversial, the quantification of the benefits and costs does raise a variety of problems, particularly regarding the value that should be attached to improved product safety.

The third principal characteristic of standards is their applicability. In particular, should we regulate products currently owned (through recall), existing product lines, or new product lines? The costs of compliance decrease as we move across these three categories. The benefits of compliance are also less for products currently owned since their future product lives tend to be less. To regulate products cost-effectively, we should set the tightest standards for new products, looser standards for newly produced products in existing product lines, and the most lenient standards for products currently in use by consumers.

By advocating more stringent regulations for new products than for existing products, I am endorsing the principle that underlies the use of "grandfather" clauses for present violators of a particular standard. Many analysts have criticized the "new source bias" of EPA regulations, whereby new plants are subjected to more stringent emissions limits than existing facilities. From an economic standpoint, the *direction* of the bias is correct; new facilities should be regulated more tightly since for any particular emissions level the marginal costs of improvements will be less.

One can, however, overdo these distinctions, as may have been the case for environmental regulations. It is in general not appropriate simply to exempt all existing products from regulation and impose very stringent regulations on new products. The regulations should be set so that the incremental cost per accident prevented is the same for all products in a group. The practical effect of such distinctions will be more stringent regulations on new products, but one cannot necessarily assume that there will be a wide disparity between the standards for new and old products.

Once standards are set, the policy problem then becomes the degree to which they are enforced. Penalties could be set at punitive levels to force compliance once violations are discovered; this is the CPSC's approach and that of other risk-regulation agencies. Alternatively, one could impose smaller fines for infractions, permitting firms to pay fines rather than alter their products' characteristics.

The imposition of more limited fines is typically viewed with abhorrence by those who consider the infraction of standards tantamount to crimes against the consumer that must not be permitted to continue. This narrow, legalistic approach ignores the quite valid economic reasons why a company might not wish to comply with a standard. If compliance costs are large, a firm will be reluctant to incur the economic losses imposed. Since compliance costs differ by firm, ideally one should set the expected penalty on the basis of the benefits of a safer product (and the probability that a noncomplying firm will be identified). If the expected costs of compliance are greater than the benefits, the firm can choose to violate the standard and pay the fine. This approach can ensure cost-effective standards on a decentralized basis.

Valuing Risk Reduction

Setting appropriate penalties or efficient standards requires the CPSC to make explicit judgments about the value of risk reduction. The most meaningful conceptual basis for assigning a value to decreases in risks is society's willingness to pay for risk reduction. To the extent that the person benefiting directly from the reduced risk has the greatest interest in this change, we can focus on his willingness to pay. This formulation does not provide a direct measure of the value of risk reduction. But it does prevent the use of wholly inappropriate values, such as medical costs and lost earnings, which may be only weakly related to willingness to pay. Since these financial measures are the norm in the regulatory analyses of federal regulatory agencies, including the CPSC, framing the valuation issue correctly is by no means inconsequential. Although the CPSC sometimes adjusts these amounts for pain and suffering, the adjustments are not based on measures of willingness to pay.

A growing literature has attempted to ascertain willingness-to-pay values through analysis of individuals' risky choices; the implications of these studies are summarized in table 6.[5] With the exception of Blomquist's study of seatbelt use, all the studies focus on wage premiums for risk.[6] Job safety has been the primary context for these analyses since information regarding workers' risks and other factors influencing income is quite extensive.

The broad range of estimates, from half a million dollars to several million dollars, is not unexpected. The risk/dollar trade-off individuals will accept varies among consumers with their particular willingness to pay for risk reduction. The search for an elusive "value of life" measure is largely misdirected; what policy makers need is information on the size and heterogeneity of such values and an assessment of their relevance to the products being regulated.

There are two principal implications of this line of research. First, we can learn a great deal about the appropriate value of risk reduction by assessing the degree to which the risk is incurred voluntarily; large risks will be incurred voluntarily by those who tend to place relatively low implicit values on their lives; consequently they should be valued less in policy evaluations. Second, evidence based on job risks indicates a value-of-life range from $500,000 for those willing to accept large risks to $2 million, $3 million, or more for those less willing to incur risks.

The empirical estimates across this range follow the pattern one might expect. Workers in high-risk jobs posing death risks on the order of 1/1,000 make choices that reflect an implicit value on their lives of roughly $500,000, as a study by Thaler and Rosen indicates.[7] Workers in typical blue-collar positions face a much lower risk—about 1/10,000 annually—and their choices display the higher implicit value of life that should be generated by the self-selection process in the labor market. Studies focusing on workers in this range have been undertaken by Smith, Leigh, and me.[8] These workers' choices reflect an implicit value of life of roughly $2 million or more. My estimates of the heterogeneity of the value-of-life estimates among all risk groups

TABLE 6
SUMMARY OF PRINCIPAL STUDIES OF DOLLAR-RISK TRADE-OFFS

Investigator	Sample	Implicit Value of Life (dollars)	Implicit Value of Nonfatal Injuries (dollars)
Blomquist	Seatbelt use, panel study of income dynamics, 1972	560,000	—
Brown	National longitudinal survey, 1967–1973	1–1.5 million	—
Leigh	Panel study of income dynamics, 1974	3.8–8.9 million*	45,000–56,000
Leigh	Quality of employment survey, 1977	4.8–8.4 million*	38,000–64,000
Olson	Current population survey, 1973	7.4 million	—
Smith	Current population survey, 1967	7.5 million	—
Smith	Current population survey, 1973	3.3 million	—

Thaler and Rosen	Survey of economic opportunity, 1967	580,000	—
Viscusi	Survey of working conditions, 1970–1971	2.9–3.9 million	23,000–34,000
Viscusi	Panel study of income dynamics, 1976	7–11 million*	32,000–35,000

NOTE: All prices are in 1982 dollars. The asterisked results for the Leigh and Viscusi studies are evaluated at the mean risk level for the sample for models in which the heterogeneity in wage-risk trade-offs was assessed.

SOURCES: Glenn Blomquist, "Value of Life Saving: Implications of Consumption Activity," *Journal of Political Economy*, vol. 87 (1979); Charles Brown, "Equalizing Differences in the Labor Market," *Quarterly Journal of Economics*, vol. 44 (1980); J. Paul Leigh, "Estimates of the Equalizing Difference Curve," *Quarterly Review of Economics and Business*, in press; Craig Olson, "An Analysis of Wage Differentials Received by Workers on Dangerous Jobs," *Journal of Human Resources*, vol. 67 (1981); Robert S. Smith, *The Occupational Safety and Health Act* (Washington, D.C.: American Enterprise Institute, 1976); Richard Thaler and Sherwin Rosen, "The Value of Saving a Life: Evidence from the Labor Market," in N. Terleckyj, ed., *Household Production and Consumption* (New York: National Bureau of Economic Research, 1976); Viscusi, *Employment Hazards*; and Viscusi, *Risk by Choice*.

are consistent with these findings for specific risk groups. A similar analysis by Leigh using comparable data sets but different specifications yielded similar results. I have also estimated the implicit value of nonfatal job injuries as between $20,000 and $30,000.

These findings do not imply that consumers will accept certain death for $2 million and certain injury for $30,000. Rather they are rates of trade-off between dollars and risk for very small incremental changes in the risk. A consumer with an implicit value of life of $1 million would, for example, be willing to pay $100 to reduce the product-related death risks he faces by 1/10,000.

Much of the debate over the appropriateness of value-of-life measures derives from the misconception that economists are valuing individuals' deaths according to their income or some other alleged "economic" measure. The controversy over these measures would not be so great if it was understood that the only issue is consumers' rate of trade-off between money and small changes in their risk.

The sophistication of the empirical studies of the value of life and the large body of supporting economic literature on these issues does not imply that we can pinpoint the precise value of these health effects. Despite their shortcomings, however, these numbers appear to be no less precise than most other components of CPSC analyses and, unlike some considerations governing CPSC policies, they have a sound methodological basis. Even policies based on imprecise benefit-cost considerations will probably be superior since relevant concerns will be raised systematically and will not be made subservient to identifying a product risk that would almost certainly be classified as unreasonable.

Estimates of the value of risk reduction will no doubt be refined in future work. But even with the current evidence, we have sufficient guidance to address cost-risk trade-offs meaningfully. Throughout this volume I advocate that such balancing of society's interests should be an explicit component of the CPSC's decisions and that policies that do not have a net beneficial effect on society should not be undertaken.

The Agenda for Policy

The principal dividend from considering the basis for intervention and alternative policy strategies before analyzing CPSC policies in detail is that this approach establishes a framework for analysis and highlights missing elements of the CPSC's activities. The usual analytic approach of assessing regulatory actions piecemeal lends itself to marginal comments on policies, but a change in the overall strategy of many regulatory agencies should be considered.

Perhaps the most fundamental implication of examining the economic foundations of CPSC policies is that our knowledge about market behavior is still rudimentary. We need to know more about the accuracy of consumers' perceptions of product risks, the extent and direction of any bias, how consumers value risk reduction, how consumers' actions respond to changes in product characteristics, and how different types of information about product risks affect consumers' risk perceptions and safety-related actions.

Even in situations in which there is a potential role for regulation, the precise form of regulation that should be adopted is not always clear. Two policies that should be ruled out are compensation schemes for product accidents and penalty systems based on product accident rates. In each case, the difficulty of monitoring consumers' behavior or the performance of the firm's overall product line will severely impede the use of these policies to promote safety. Product liability remedies have similar shortcomings.

The most promising policy options are an information-based strategy and a standards-penalty system. These policies should promote risk reduction only until the cost of the incremental decrease in risk just equals society's willingness to pay for extra safety. It is this kind of explicit balancing of benefits and costs that distinguishes the ideal risk-regulation policies from the modes the CPSC has chosen to pursue. These inadequacies can best be considered in the context of the agency's operations, which I address in the following chapters.

Notes

1. This individual response is derived for the automobile safety case by Sam Peltzman, "The Effects of Automobile Safety Regulation," *Journal of Political Economy*, vol. 83 (1975), pp. 677–725; and for the job safety case by W. Kip Viscusi, *Employment Hazards: An Investigation of Market Performance* (Cambridge, Mass.: Harvard University Press, 1979). Few restrictive assumptions are required to generate these results.

2. The underlying theoretical analysis is provided in Michael Spence, "Monopoly, Quality, and Regulation," *Bell Journal of Economics*, vol. 6 (1975), pp. 417–29.

3. The discussion in this paragraph is based on the work reported in W. Kip Viscusi and Charles O'Connor, "Adaptive Responses to Job Risk Information," Center for the Study of Business Regulation, Duke University, Working Paper No. 83-9 (1983).

4. A lucid discussion of these issues can be found in Michael Spence,

Market Signaling (Cambridge, Mass.: Harvard University Press, 1974); and Spence, "Consumer Misperceptions, Product Failure, Producer Liability," *Review of Economic Studies,* vol. 44 (1977), pp. 561–72.

5. Table 6 is reasonably comprehensive, but the discussion of the studies and their policy implications is not intended to be complete. For more extensive surveys, see Martin Bailey, *Reducing Risks to Life: Measurement of the Benefits* (Washington, D.C.: American Enterprise Institute, 1980); Robert S. Smith, "Compensating Differentials and Public Policy: A Review," *Industrial and Labor Relations Review,* vol. 32 (1979), pp.339–52; and W. Kip Viscusi, *Risk by Choice: Regulating Health and Safety in the Workplace* (Cambridge, Mass.: Harvard University Press, 1983).

6. Glenn Blomquist, "Value of Life Saving: Implications of Consumption Activity," *Journal of Political Economy,* vol. 87 (1979), pp. 540–58.

7. See Richard Thaler and Sherwin Rosen, "The Value of Saving a Life: Evidence from the Labor Market," in N. Terleckyj, ed., *Household Production and Consumption* (New York: National Bureau of Economic Research, 1976).

8. See Robert Smith, *The Occupational Safety and Health Act* (Washington, D.C.: American Enterprise Institute, 1976); J. Paul Leigh, "Estimates of the Equalizing Difference Curve," *Quarterly Review of Economics and Business,* in press; and Viscusi, *Risk by Choice.*

3

The Regulatory Strategy
of the CPSC

Overview of the CPSC

The Consumer Product Safety Commission has one of the most extensive mandates of any risk-regulation agency. In many respects, it can be viewed as the product market counterpart to the Occupational Safety and Health Administration (OSHA). Both agencies exercise broad responsibility over diverse health and safety risks throughout the economy.

The CPSC was established in October 1972 in the midst of the flurry of new risk-regulation agencies authorized in the early 1970s. Congress gave the new agency general responsibilities for product safety. The CPSC was entrusted with safety functions formerly scattered through the federal government. It assumed functions under the Hazardous Substances Act (formerly administered by the Department of Health, Education, and Welfare, the Department of Commerce, and the Federal Trade Commission), the Poison Prevention Packaging Act of 1970 (formerly administered by the Department of Health, Education, and Welfare), and the Refrigerator Safety Act (formerly administered by the Department of Commerce and the Federal Trade Commission).[1]

Despite the apparent breadth of its mandate, the CPSC was explicitly prohibited from regulating a group of the most hazardous products, which continued to be overseen by other agencies. Specifically excluded from coverage were tobacco and tobacco products, motor vehicles and motor vehicle equipment, pesticides, aircraft, boats, food, drugs, and cosmetics.[2] These products are regulated by other agencies, such as the National Highway Traffic Safety Administration and the Food and Drug Administration. The excluded products are among those with the highest risks. From the outset the CPSC was a

TABLE 7
ACCIDENTAL DEATH RATES AND DISTRIBUTION OF ACCIDENTS BY TYPE, 1981

Type	Death Rate (per 100,000)	Percentage of All Accidents
Motor vehicle	22.2	51
Work	5.4	13
Home	9.2	21
Public, non–motor-vehicle	8.5	20

NOTE: Percentages add to more than 100 because of rounding and, more important, because some accidents may fall in more than one category.

SOURCES: National Safety Council, *Accident Facts* (Chicago: National Safety Council, 1982), p. 13; and calculations by the author.

catchall regulatory agency for products not already covered by a product-specific regulatory body.

The scope of the CPSC's authority can best be illustrated in the context of the distribution of accidents. As the summary of accidental deaths by category in table 7 indicates, the majority of accidents are related to motor vehicles. Home accidents, the next largest category, account for more accidental deaths than work accidents. The CPSC has a potentially larger role than OSHA.

One cannot conclude, however, that the work environment is necessarily safer than the home. More time is spent at home than at work. Of greater importance, the age distributions of people at home and at work are different. If we exclude motor vehicle accidents (which account for the bulge in accidents among those in their late teens), the age groups with high accident rates are at both tails of the population. Persons under the age of four and those over the age of sixty-five are most prone to fatal accidents. Since these groups have low employment rates, the home accident rate is boosted accordingly.

The data on the causes of accidents imply a roughly similar scope of CPSC authority (see table 8). Because of both its legislative mandate and the nature of accidents, the CPSC can have little effect on motor vehicle accidents, falls, drownings, accidents with firearms, or poisoning by gases and vapors. The remaining categories account for one-fourth of all accidental deaths, not all of which are subject to the CPSC's influence. Ingestions of toys by infants, for example, can be a target of CPSC policies, but choking on food cannot. In addition,

TABLE 8
Distribution of Accidental Deaths by Cause, 1981

Cause	Death Rate (per 100,000)	Percentage of All Accidents
Motor vehicle accidents	22.2	51
Falls	5.1	12
Drowning	2.6	6
Fires and burns	2.1	5
Suffocation—ingested object	1.4	3
Poisoning by solids and liquids	1.1	3
Firearms	0.8	2
Poisoning by gases and vapors	0.8	2
All other	7.1	16
Total accidents	43.2	100

Sources: National Safety Council, *Accident Facts*, pp. 6–7; and calculations by the author.

many of these categories include both home and work accidents, which are affected by both CPSC and OSHA policies.

Perhaps the best measure of the CPSC's jurisdiction is obtained from the CPSC's estimate that 30,000 people are killed annually in accidents involving consumer products. This tally constitutes about 30 percent of all fatal accidents.[3] Since the role of consumer products in determining accidents may be quite minor and CPSC regulations can reduce only a portion of the product-related accidents, the scope for actually reducing accidents through CPSC policy is much less.

The limited extent to which the CPSC can influence accidents involving consumer products can be assessed by inspecting the leading product accident categories summarized in table 9. Stairs are the most hazardous product, although the "product" classification here must be interpreted rather broadly. Apart from following OSHA's lead in regulating stair width and placement of handrails, there is not much that can be done to regulate this product. (The CPSC is, however, working with architects to develop a possible regulation for stairs.) Moreover, unlike other consumer products, stairs are usually an integral part of a building's structure and not mass produced or sold in stores. Their decentralized production makes them more difficult to regulate.

Five of the next seven risky products are related to sports. Although bicycles can be regulated, as CPSC has done, any effect on

TABLE 9
The Ten Products Involved in the Most Injuries, 1981

Product Group	Injuries (thousands)
Stairs, steps, ramps, and landings	763
Bicycles and bicycle accessories	518
Baseball	478
Football	470
Basketball	434
Nails, carpet tacks, screws, and thumbtacks	244
Chairs, sofas, and sofa beds	236
Skating	225
Nonglass tables	225
Glass doors, windows, and panels	208

Source: U.S. Consumer Product Safety Commission (CPSC), *Annual Report* (Washington, D.C., 1982), pp. 22ff.

safety will be marginal. Nails and tacks no doubt will remain a source of injury so long as they have sharp points.

The risks from chairs and sofas, chiefly fire hazards, can be reduced through flame-resistant materials. Nonglass tables pose risks to those who fall onto them, particularly children, but except for requiring tables to have rounded edges, there is little the CPSC can do to affect their safety. Glass doors and windows pose often severe laceration risks for those who fall through the glass. The CPSC already has in place a standard intended to reduce this risk through glazing and tempering.

For the most hazardous product groups, the potential for CPSC influence appears to be quite minor. Apart from outright bans on activities—such as abolishing the national pastime, baseball—the incremental effect of any CPSC policy, however well designed, will be at most a moderate reduction in injuries rather than an elimination of hazards.

For risks within the agency's jurisdiction, Congress charged the CPSC with the duty "to protect the public against unreasonable risks of injury associated with consumer products."[4] This "unreasonable risk" concept is dominant in the agency's enabling legislation and has governed its subsequent operations. While possessing some superficial appeal—who, after all, could oppose regulating a risk that is unreasonable?—this concept does not provide either a well-defined or a meaningful basis for policy.

First, the interpretation of risk is unclear. Do we measure risk by the total number of injuries, the probability that a consumer will be injured by a product in any given year, or the probability of injury adjusted for the frequency of the product's use? Although the final measure is most meaningful, it is the measure of total adverse health outcomes that dominates the CPSC's policy approach.

Second, and more fundamentally, *the level of the risk alone is not a sufficient basis for government intervention*, however one chooses to define the measure of risk. As I indicated in the previous chapter, *what matters is the existence of some inadequacy in the market*; the presence of a nonzero risk by itself tells us nothing about whether intervention is warranted. Although the Consumer Product Safety Act also noted the "inability of users to anticipate risks and to safeguard themselves adequately,"[5] which is a market inadequacy, these concerns are in addition to those embodied in the unreasonable risk criterion. For all supporting analyses for CPSC standards, the existence of a risk and CPSC's capacity to alter that risk serve as the primary basis for intervention. The presence of any inadequacy in market processes or its importance has not been at the forefront of policy decisions.

The CPSC's focus on "unreasonable risks" distinguishes it only slightly from other agencies, such as OSHA, that deal with "significant risks" or other risk-based concerns.[6] The Food and Drug Administration makes a similar distinction, focusing on "substantial" risks. In each case, some measure of the risk, not the overall merits of the policy, is of paramount concern.

This is not to say that the CPSC's policies are conceived as being independent of cost considerations. Risk reductions that are clearly infeasible, such as eliminating the risks of baseball or of chainsaws, are not pursued when consumer demand for the product is strong and there are no good substitutes. Such concerns are not completely independent of making cost-risk trade-offs, but these trade-offs are recognized only in extreme instances. In addition, the CPSC is now legally required to balance the likelihood and severity of injuries against the costs of risk reduction.[7]

The degree to which the CPSC undertakes such balancing is not altogether different from that of other regulatory agencies, which also are primarily concerned with regulation's effect on risk reduction. OSHA is also subject to legal constraints; it cannot impose regulatory costs unless they produce a "significant" reduction in risk.[8] Moreover, whereas the CPSC focuses on the availability of highly valued product types, OSHA is likewise concerned with extreme effects on cost; it attempts to avoid regulations that lead to the shutdown of firms. OSHA's affordability criterion may go even further than the CPSC's weighing of costs since the CPSC often bans products altogether, causing the cessation of firms' operations, provided that consumers have a suitable substitute. In short, the forces that dictate the CPSC's actions are not starkly different from those that drive the policies of other risk-regulation agencies.

In its scale of operations, the CPSC ranks in the lower tier of risk-regulation agencies. Table 10 summarizes the budgets and staff size of the principal federal agencies engaged in risk regulation. The Environmental Protection Agency (EPA) has by far the largest budget and staff, and OSHA is second. The staff of the CPSC is roughly comparable in size to that of the National Highway Traffic Safety Administration.

The CPSC's administrative structure is also similar to those of other regulatory commissions. The CPSC is an independent regulatory commission headed by five commissioners appointed by the president, with the advice and consent of the Senate.[9] It consequently has a quasi-judicial format, in which the five commissioners must interpret the appropriate application of the body of law it administers. If the administrative task required only that they interpret well-defined regulatory criteria impartially, this structure might be appropriate. One should note, however, that the political appointment of the commissioners is certain to affect the policy outcomes. Effective regulation of product safety requires primarily an ability to assess the benefits and costs of regulatory alternatives, which can be viewed as

TABLE 10
BUDGET AND STAFF OF MAJOR RISK-REGULATION AGENCIES, 1982

Agency	Estimated Budget (thousands of dollars)	Total Staff
Consumer Product Safety Commission	33,983	697
Environmental Protection Agency	5,799,414	11,028
Food and Drug Administration	362,695	7,056
National Highway Traffic Safety Administration	312,803	791
Nuclear Regulatory Commission	484,200	3,396
Occupational Safety and Health Administration	235,330	2,925

SOURCE: U.S. Office of Management and Budget, *The Budget of the United States Government, Fiscal Year 1982* (Washington, D.C., 1982).

rationality in economic terms, rather than simply assess the implications of the law. The economic analysis division, however, plays a subsidiary role in the agency operations.

The independent status of the CPSC also makes it immune from the White House regulatory oversight process. Since President Reagan sacrificed the explicit authority to intervene publicly in CPSC rule makings when he abolished the Council on Wage and Price Stability, there is no formal review of the CPSC's actions by the Office of Management and Budget to comment on whether they are beneficial. Previous reviews did not ensure efficient regulation because the council's comments were not binding, but they did provide a White House contribution to the regulatory process and information that was often used in judicial proceedings. Under the Reagan administration regulatory oversight has become a more binding review process, but only for executive branch agencies. Although the present system is not ideal, its focus on the benefits and costs of regulation and the existence of an external check on regulatory policy are both desirable features of the rule-making process.

The commission structure has an additional deficiency unrelated to the emphasis that the agency should have. A commission intrinsically embodies divided responsibility and no additional accountability, except through the courts and the Congress. A five-member commission diffuses an agency's leadership and tends to create more muddled lines of authority than the structure of an executive agency. This criticism of the commission structure pertains not only to the CPSC but to other commissions as well. Whether or not the relatively unwieldy commission format should be adopted depends on other considerations. If, for example, an agency's mission were solely to serve a quasi-judicial function (which the CPSC's is not), a commission format might be desirable.

Political considerations may also influence the effectiveness of a commission. Because policies will be governed by the commission chairman and the majority on any decision, there is less incentive to exercise care in each appointment than if a single administrator were being selected. As a consequence, commissions tend to include some of the less able political appointees, particularly commissions, such as the CPSC, that do not play a dominant role in regulation.

The independence of the commissioners reduces their accountability and may further affect the quality of their performance by eliminating the work incentives that arise from the possibility of being replaced. Although the offsetting advantage is that the commissioners are less subject to political influences, in practice those political influences are often not sinister efforts to undermine an agency's objec-

39

tives but signals that its policies have gone awry. Most industries voicing complaints about regulations during the Carter administration, for example, either had legitimate grievances or were accurately identifying instances of large regulatory burdens. The regulations that were subsequently relaxed almost invariably were those shown to be undesirable on benefit-cost grounds. They had previously been opposed unsuccessfully by the Council on Wage and Price Stability and the economic staff of the Council of Economic Advisers, which claimed that they were inefficient and ill conceived. The intrusion of "political" factors in such cases may enable policies to be more responsive and better designed than those undertaken irrespective of such concerns.

The ultimate effect of the CPSC hinges on the resources it commands, not simply on its structure. The budgetary history has deviated sharply from the usual pattern of steadily increasing expenditures. CPSC budgetary outlays reached a peak of $45 million in fiscal year 1980; the budget was slashed to $33 million in FY 1982.[10] The number of staff positions also dropped from a peak of 914 in FY 1975 to 697 in FY 1982. This involuntary cutback reflects both congressional dissatisfaction with the commission and recent budgetary stringency.

The long-run trend in actual expenditures and staff, which was fairly steadily downward throughout the FY 1977 to FY 1982 period, is summarized in table 11. Even the comparative budgetary stability

TABLE 11
CPSC BUDGET AND STAFF, FISCAL YEARS 1973–1982

Fiscal Year	Budgetary Outlays (millions of dollars)	Staff
1973	0.02	579
1974	18.7	780
1975	34.2	884
1976	38.4	890
1977	39.9	914
1978	40.1	897
1979	39.3	879
1980	45.1	880
1981	43.9	880
1982	33.0	697

SOURCE: U.S. Office of Management and Budget, various budgetary publications. The updated FY 1982 figures are from CPSC, *Annual Report* (1982).

through FY 1982 is somewhat misleading. Most risk-regulation agencies experienced rapid growth during this period. The absence of a major expansion in the commission's administrative structure is, at the very least, a signal that Congress did not view an expansion of the agency's efforts as a productive use of federal funds.

Policy Options

The Consumer Product Safety Act had four principal purposes:

1. to protect the public against unreasonable risks of injury associated with consumer products
2. to assist consumers in evaluating the comparative safety of consumer products
3. to develop uniform safety standards
4. to promote research and investigation into the causes and prevention of product-related deaths, illnesses, and injuries[11]

The overridding objective was to prevent "unreasonable risks" and to do so in a manner that is "in the public interest."[12] Although the explicit criteria for policy design are much more extensive than this myopic risk criterion, the agency's emphasis has been on policies motivated by the risk rather than by the net effect on society.

Besides being given the general responsibility for consumer protection, the CPSC was explicitly given the tasks of providing consumer information, setting standards, and undertaking research. In practice, its actions have concentrated not so much on these three obligations as on bans and recalls undertaken for the broader purpose of protecting the consumer. Standards have been the most frequently used of the three policy options detailed in the legislation. The provision of consumer information has played a relatively minor role. Product safety research is not a separate agency function but has consisted of providing the supporting information for more direct forms of regulatory intervention. The stated purposes do not accurately reflect the emphasis that the CPSC has in fact placed on different activities. A major shortcoming of the agency's performance is that consumer information has not been given the prominence outlined in the statement of its purpose.

The policy instruments available are quite diverse, including standards, bans, recalls, seizure of hazardous products, voluntary standards, certification and labeling, and an indirect effect on exports through other government policies.[13] The first of these options, standards, serves as the principal policy tool of most risk-regulation agencies and, from the legislation, might be expected, along with con-

41

sumer information, to be the dominant CPSC policy. In practice, standards play a role subsidiary to that of bans and recalls.

If we exclude the CPSC's broad ad hoc authority to take actions against hazardous products, which is discussed below, the commission's principal policies fall into three broad categories: standards, bans, and seizure of products posing imminent hazards. Product safety standards must "be reasonably necessary to prevent or reduce an unreasonable risk of injury associated with such product" and should "be expressed in terms of performance requirements" whenever feasible.[14] The criteria for standard setting are discussed in greater detail below; the "unreasonable risk" and "reasonably necessary" requirements are the most important. Product bans can be viewed as an extreme form of standard in which the CPSC cannot simply prevent "unreasonable risk" through a standard for certain product characteristics but finds it necessary to prevent the use of the product since "no feasible consumer product safety standard . . . would adequately protect the public."[15] The CPSC can ban or recall hazardous products not covered by existing standards or bans when appropriate.

Each of these policies entails a rule-making proceeding either in advance of the policy or after it for imminent hazards. In practice, the CPSC has never initiated a rule making after an imminent hazard action, because the problems have not been industrywide. The risk-regulation proposals of most agencies must meet only very loose legal criteria. The executive branch agencies have been constrained largely by the requirements of the White House regulatory oversight process. The CPSC no longer comes under formal presidential oversight, but it does have a series of formal requirements imposed by its legislation that are more stringent than those faced by most other risk-regulation agencies.

The CPSC legislation requires that the commission "make appropriate findings" on the following issues before promulgating a rule: "the degree and nature of the risk of injury . . ., the approximate number of consumer products . . . subject to the rule, the need of the public for the consumer products . . ., and any means of achieving the objective of the order while minimizing adverse effects on competition."[16] These informational requirements are augmented by three criteria that must be met before promulgating a rule: (1) the rule must be "reasonably necessary to eliminate or reduce an unreasonable risk of injury"; (2) it must be "in the public interest"; and (3) a ban must not be used if a standard would "adequately protect the public from the unreasonable risk of injury."[17] The 1981 amendments to the Consumer Product Safety Act strengthened these requirements by ordering the agency to prepare findings that contain "a description of the

42

potential benefits and potential costs of the rule, including costs and benefits that cannot be quantified in monetary terms, and the identification of those likely to receive the benefits and bear the costs." [18]

No formal benefit-cost trade-off is required, but the commission is required to gather some obviously relevant data, to regulate "unreasonable risks," and to do so in a manner that promotes the "public interest." The "unreasonable risk" criterion has proved dominant in CPSC decisions, but the "public interest" provision may be more consequential to the extent that all the policy's effects, not simply its effect on risks, affect the public interest. In this respect the CPSC has a much more flexible mandate than that of most other risk-regulation agencies.

Also playing a pivotal role are the closely related guidelines for CPSC priorities, which have broad applicability to the agency's actions. The CPSC policy statement lists risk-related concerns as the first three priorities: the frequency and severity of injuries, the causes of injuries and their amenability to policy influence, and chronic illnesses and future injuries. [19] Fourth on the priority list are the costs and benefits of CPSC actions, but the commission disavows a benefit-cost test because of alleged "analytical uncertainties that complicate matters and militate against reliance on single numerical expressions." Hence the commission cannot commit itself to priorities based solely on the preliminary benefit-cost comparisons that will be available at the stage of priority setting or to any one form of comparison, such as net benefits or benefit-cost ratios. [20] This language does not, however, rule out benefit-cost analysis as a primary tool for policy analysis and design. All that is required by the statement is that "preliminary" benefit-cost analyses not be the "sole" basis for decisions. Presumably formal recognition of the policy trade-offs through benefit-cost analysis could be instrumental in determining the ultimate policy decision. The priority list concludes with three additional risk-related criteria: the unforeseen nature of the risk, the vulnerability of the population at risk, and the probability of exposure to the hazard. [21]

Before criticizing the CPSC's approach, we should put these guidelines in perspective since even seriously flawed criteria for evaluating policy may be a significant improvement over most agencies' behavior. Perhaps most striking is the diverse relevant information that is gathered and the consideration of benefit-cost trade-offs, though not in a prominent manner. This emphasis is also reflected in the public position of the agency. Former CPSC Chairman Susan King, for example, did not make the usual ritualistic commitment to total risk reduction but noted that a "risk-free society is not attainable." [22] In a description of a preliminary analysis of sofa flammability standards, the CPSC assessed the cost per life saved. More recently it has solicited advice on the appropriate values to be placed on life and health.[23] These actions are remarkably innovative when compared with those of other risk-regulation agencies. Although narrower concerns have dominated policies, the fact that some risk-regulation issues have begun to be raised in an analytically sound fashion is perhaps the agency's most distinctive achievement.

Nevertheless, the CPSC has fallen far short of reliance on a proper economic test and continues to focus on factors related to "unreasonable risk." The explicit disavowal of the accuracy of a benefit-cost test has led to regulatory analyses that summarize some relevant effects but do not put them in a form useful for policy design. The analysis of the cost per life saved of sofa flammability standards is not the norm, and it was presented as a test case of cost-effectiveness analysis for illustrative purposes. More typically there is no explicit benefit-cost or cost-effectiveness calculation but simply a partial description of some relevant effects. These shortcomings reflect not inadequacies in the analyses by the CPSC economics staff but rather a failure of the CPSC commissioners to give economic analysis more prominence. The economic analysis is only a small component of the briefing package used by the commissioners in making their decisions. In contrast, the regulatory analyses now undertaken by executive branch agencies are much more comprehensive, in large part because those agencies are subject to formal scrutiny by the OMB.

For its lead paint standard, for example, the CPSC claims that there is "an unreasonable risk of lead poisoning in children associated with lead content of over 0.06 percent in paints and coatings" and that the rule will raise the cost of paint by five to ten cents a gallon.[24] Such assessments may be accurate, and on balance the standard may have been desirable. But the information generated by the CPSC provides little basis for a sound policy decision. What we would like to know is whether a ban on paint containing lead will produce total improvements in health valued more than the total costs imposed. To learn this, we need an assessment of the effect of the lead paint standard on the lead levels in children's blood, the relation of lead exposure levels to individual health, the severity and overall value of the effects on health, and the *total* cost to firms and consumers of banning this product, not simply the cents per gallon.

In the lead paint standard and other instances in which the underlying analysis was deficient, the commission may nevertheless have made the correct policy decision. But in the absence of such an analysis, it is less likely that decisions made on the basis of whim or risk considerations will be as sound as those based on an informed assessment of the policy's merits. The deficiencies in the CPSC's regulatory analyses are explored further in chapter 6.

These inadequacies in the development of CPSC policies stem from the lack of a full commitment by the agency to economic analysis as a basis for decision. Various numbers are generated to comply with the CPSC legislation and policy statements, but these are largely pro forma. What matters for regulatory decisions is the discussion of the product risk coupled with the apparent presumption that all risks are unreasonable if they can conceivably be affected by CPSC policies without depriving consumers of a uniquely attractive product.

The CPSC's skepticism regarding a benefit-cost test derives from our alleged inability to assess properly the value of various effects on health. The conceptual basis for valuing these effects is well established. The values should hinge on consumers' willingness to pay for the risk reduction, not the CPSC's measure, which is dominated by medical costs and forgone earnings. The CPSC falls into a more general pattern of agencies that do not wish to value human life explicitly but actually do so in their assessment of accident costs—the direct financial burdens of medical care and forgone earnings. These measures typically understate consumers' willingness to pay for risk reduction by roughly a factor of ten. Somewhat ironically, the reluctance of the CPSC and other risk-regulation agencies to value willingness to pay to reduce risks of fatalities leads to severe underestimates of the actual economic value.

The CPSC's failure to incorporate benefit-cost criteria in its priority setting pertains not only to standards and bans but also to other actions. Recalls and bans of products already subject to explicit CPSC regulation are based indirectly on the requirements imposed on agency rule makings since the basis for the actions is an existing rule. Certification and labeling policies are also the subject of formal rule makings; for example, the standard for walk-behind power lawn mowers even specifies the size, shape, and color of the warning "Danger—Keep Hands and Feet Away." [25] Voluntary standards are scrutinized less formally and must be complementary to other CPSC actions. [26] The 1981 amendments to the Consumer Product Safety Act, however, require increased care by the CPSC in assessing the effects of voluntary standards.

What is by far the most important policy tool used by the CPSC— its broad recall authority—is also immune from the requirements of standard rule-making proceedings since no regulations need be promulgated. Indeed, I maintain in the following chapter that the emphasis on this policy derives largely from this exemption from the rule-making process and the discretion it gives the agency. Section 15 of the Consumer Product Safety Act establishes the authority for the commission to require notification of a product defect, modification of a product, replacement of a product, and refunds of the purchase price. Recalls and corrective actions are permitted in two cases: (1) violations of existing rules *or "(2) a product defect which . . . creates a substantial risk of injury to the consumer."* [27] Since determination that a risk is "substantial" is very vaguely defined, the second provision in effect gives the commission free reign to regulate products almost at will even in the absence of preexisting standards to guide companies' actions and no accountability in a formal rule-making proceeding. So long as the section 15 authority remains, the CPSC can regulate products on an ad hoc basis without promulgating formal regulations. As a result, the strictures imposed by the policy evaluation criteria can be regarded as inessential boilerplate.

Enforcement Mechanisms

Although product bans tend to be intrinsically absolute, safety standards need not take the form of rigid constraints on product characteristics. The CPSC could presumably penalize firms for hazardous products, giving them an incentive to produce safe goods and consumers an incentive to purchase less hazardous products. The objective would be not to eliminate products or certain product characteristics but to work through the market to promote efficient levels of safety, while maintaining the benefits offered by products of diverse quality.

The commission has not opted for this approach. Instead, it has followed the familiar tradition of requiring compliance with its standards. To promote compliance, the CPSC can impose record-keeping requirements, undertake plant inspections, and seek civil and criminal penalties or injunctive enforcement.[28] Moreover, all firms remain subject to common law liability irrespective of their compliance.[29] Table 12 summarizes the enforcement statistics for FY 1982.

The CPSC estimates that since 1973 its recalls alone have affected 176 million items, many of which involved the same product.[30] The 15,000 inspections, sample collections, and recall effectiveness checks may seem impressive but are dwarfed by the scope of the agency's responsibility.

The admittedly moderate level of inspections has led to few substantive actions. There were fewer than 100 adverse actions of all kinds, including injunctions, seizures, consent agreements, and voluntary compliance agreements. Almost two-thirds of the total were voluntary compliance agreements. The more stringent actions also are

TABLE 12

CPSC COMPLIANCE ACTIVITIES, FISCAL YEAR 1982

Recall effectiveness checks	8,409
Inspections	4,120
Sample collections	2,772
Voluntary compliance agreements	62
Injunctions	13
Civil penalties	12
Seizures	6
Consent agreements	5

SOURCE: CPSC, *Annual Report*, pt. 2 (Washington, D.C., 1981), p. 216.

quite moderate; eight of the twelve civil penalty actions were for unstable refuse bins, with penalties ranging from $1,000 to $4,000.[31]

The almost negligible sanctions might lead one to predict widespread noncompliance due to the lack of effective financial incentives. The commission has the ability, however, to impose ever-escalating financial burdens and to undertake actions that will give adverse publicity to noncomplying firms. Moreover, although the number of affected products is great, the number of CPSC rules is not especially large, so that the enforcement task is narrowly defined. Finally, product lines tend to be quite similar and can be readily inspected. Whereas full enforcement of an OSHA standard in all cases would require inspection of millions of workplaces, one can ascertain whether the thousands of Bayer aspirin bottles sold each year comply with the protective cap requirements by inspecting a sample bottle from each bottle size.

The CPSC's compliance data are suggestive in ascertaining whether the paucity of penalty actions is a consequence of a high rate of compliance or of an enforcement effort so ineffective that violations are overlooked. CPSC estimates for several standards indicate substantial but incomplete compliance: 5–10 percent noncompliance with a 1978 refuse bin requirement, 5 percent noncompliance with 1980 packaging requirements for acetaminophen preparations, and a decrease in noncompliance with carpet flammability standards (issued primarily in 1975), down from a one-third noncompliance rate two years earlier.[32]

These selective case studies and the statistics generated by the enforcement effort appear to indicate substantial compliance. Since the enforcement effort itself is not stringent, the reason for its success seems to be largely the ease with which safety-related attributes can be assessed. In some cases, such as carpet flammability, tests are required, but for the most part certification of compliance requires monitoring the presence of warning signs or safety guards or the spacing of crib bars.

If it is the ease of monitoring compliance that has led to the apparent success of the enforcement effort, the more fundamental issue is whether consumers can also readily monitor safety-related attributes. Many safety characteristics regulated by the CPSC are readily observable. In instances in which extensive testing is required, the safety rating could be provided to consumers. Carpet materials, for example, could be given standardized grades for flammability. The responsibility for monitoring observable attributes could be transferred entirely to consumers, and the CPSC could provide additional information to consumers in instances in which the safety characteristic cannot be readily observed.

Such a grading system offers greater flexibility since the risk posed by a product attribute varies among consumers. The most noteworthy case is that of flammable fabrics. Upholstery materials that have better flammability ratings also tend to embody synthetic substances that emit very toxic fumes when burned. Nonsmoking consumers may face a lower risk from the more flammable fabrics, whereas smokers' risks will be reduced if flame-resistant materials are used. A fundamental policy issue is whether a greater risk and expense should be imposed on nonsmokers to protect careless smokers, particularly since smoking is voluntary. Grading systems that leave leeway for consumers' choices do not encounter such difficulties.

Product Hazard Information

The Consumer Product Safety Act directed the CPSC not only to regulate unreasonable risks but also to establish a product safety data base and "to collect, investigate, and disseminate injury data, and information, relating to the causes and prevention of death, injury, and illness associated with consumer products."[33] In practice the data base, though not created to serve primarily in support of standards and recall policies, simply provides the quantitative backing for the determination that a risk is unreasonable.

Other risk-regulation agencies gather data, the chief among these being OSHA's injury and illness reports. Discussion of these datagathering efforts is usually relegated to footnotes since they are usually an innocuous component of the overall administrative structure. For the CPSC the data base provides more than substantive filler for its annual reports. The targets for CPSC actions are selected on the basis of these data. Equally important, the nature of the CPSC's approach to risk regulation is revealed in quite stark terms through the data it chooses to collect.

Before considering the specifics of the CPSC system, we will find it instructive to ask what data we would desire if we could acquire full information costlessly. Ideally we would like to know the probability of different adverse health outcomes associated with different products. The products should be defined as narrowly as possible by manufacturer, product line, and age. The probabilities should be adjusted to reflect the frequency of use; thus we want to know how often the consumer uses the product causing the injury and how often the product is used without injury. Finally, the role of individual actions and personal characteristics in contributing to the risk should be ascertained, since product safety policies as now designed will primarily alter the contribution of the product to the injury, not the contribution of the user.

Clearly, many of these pieces of information—especially the role of consumers' actions—are difficult to assess reliably. But this perfect-information yardstick is useful in distinguishing whether we are gathering the right data imperfectly or are simply generating the wrong kind of data.

The CPSC's National Electronic Injury Surveillance System (NEISS) has been in operation since mid-1972, and calendar year data for product injuries are available beginning in 1973. The system began through a merger of the data collection efforts of the FDA's National Injury Surveillance System and the National Commission on Product Safety's Hospital Emergency Room Injury Reporting System. NEISS provides a time series on product-related injuries for approximately 1,000 product groups (such as vacuum cleaners). The information consists of the general product type, the disposition of the injured consumer (for example, whether or not he died), the consumer's personal characteristics (for example, age), and miscellaneous background information (for example, the state in which the injury occurred). The data come from a sample of emergency departments in hospitals and are extrapolated to generate a national average. In effect, NEISS primarily constructs an estimate of total injuries by product type from data on selected hospital admissions.

Even if NEISS were implemented perfectly, the system would be less than ideal. The major shortcoming is not the data that are collected but the information that is not gathered. Most important is that NEISS measures not the probability of injury but the total number of injuries. There is no measure of intensity of use by the injured con-

49

sumer. Because this is a self-selected sample based on hospital admissions, there is no information on consumers who use the product often without adverse consequences.

By basing its regulatory analyses and policies on total injury data rather than injury probabilities, the CPSC may actually be increasing the risk to consumers by regulating products that are used quite frequently and may pose a negligible risk of injury. Hazardous products regulated by the CPSC generally pose a risk far below 1/10,000 per year, which is the average job risk faced by American workers. Once consumers substitute other activities for products that pose annual death risks on the order of 1/100,000 or less—as many regulated products do—their overall exposure to risk may increase. Focusing on total injury data does not provide a sound basis for even a myopic policy of promoting risk reduction.

This inadequacy is not inherent. There are various ways to gather information on the intensity of use. The CPSC could collect product sales information or ask injured consumers how often they used the product. Industry trade associations often have such information, and the U.S. Department of Commerce collects total dollar shipment data for broad product categories that can be used. The size of the population of users can also be monitored. Knowing the number of children in various age groups, for example, can enable us to assess better the extent to which the decline in injuries associated with baby cribs is due to a CPSC standard or simply to a reduction in the number of exposed children. These data should be gathered on a continuing basis, not just for products already selected as targets for CPSC intervention. In many instances, currently available information is sufficient to put the risk in probability terms (without adjusting for frequency of use) since the number of product injuries and the number of products of a particular type involved are frequently calculated in CPSC regulatory analyses. Even partial conversions of injury data into use-adjusted probabilities would enable the CPSC to target its policies more effectively.

A second difficulty is whether any self-selected sample such as this can be truly representative. The uninjured and those injured but not admitted to hospital emergency rooms are excluded, and consumers who are killed may have been involved in accidents whose causes become more difficult to ascertain once they are dead. It is also conceivable that a hospital in the NEISS sample may be more likely to identify an accident as product related because the hospital is in the sample, even though the product was only peripherally involved in the accident.

Even with no bias in the classifications, policy makers should not use the system to evaluate narrowly defined product categories, as they have in the past. The current data appear to be reliable only for very broad product groups. Two deficiencies are most salient. First, many of the product group cells are quite small, and it is not possible to extrapolate them reliably to yield a national average. In 1980, for example, one accident with an electric water heater led to an estimate of 121 accidents nationally, and one accident with a burglar alarm was extrapolated to a national estimate of 32 injuries. Such refined distinctions based on a sample of a single injury are not particularly meaningful and should not serve as the basis for policy design. Much broader product categories are needed for valid inferences.

The second deficiency is that even for relatively large product groups the problems of small sample size become compounded by classification difficulties. Table 13 presents total national injuries with extension ladders, which were selected because the problems illustrated by this product were representative, not aberrational. The injury estimates fluctuate wildly, with no apparent trend. Part of the difficulty is that even for a product associated with a moderately large number of injury reports (forty-three in 1979), the sample size is still too small to make precise inferences possible. Perhaps more important is the large capricious element in the classifications. An injured consumer may complain that he fell from his ladder but may not give complete information to the hospital, or the hospital may not properly record the information. An accident with an extension ladder could be recorded in one of the following five NEISS categories: stepladder,

TABLE 13
NEISS Data on Extension Ladder Injuries, 1974–1981

Year	National Injury Estimate
1974	406
1975	4,385
1976	2,162
1977	1,987
1978	1,142
1979	2,978
1980	1,119
1981	2,398

Source: CPSC, NEISS computer printouts.

ladders (not specified), straight ladders, step stools, and other ladders.

NEISS data should be relied on only for very comprehensive categories (such as ladders) to avoid classification problems and sample size problems. Although extension ladder injuries more than doubled from 1980 to 1981, for example, the number of all injuries with ladders was 99,000 in 1981 and 89,000 in 1980. This limitation of the NEISS system points up its weakness as a basis for regulating narrowly defined product categories and products involved in few injuries. The CPSC's practice of basing many policies on only one or two years' escalation in accidents makes regulatory policy susceptible to random swings in accident data.

If one uses the data at their current level of aggregation or at a much broader level of aggregation, the policy will not be targeted at the particular hazardous products but at all products in the group. What we would like to know is not simply the general product involved but the contribution of the particular product to the accident. What were the product's make, its age, and the way in which it was used by the consumer? The CPSC has a second system within NEISS for selected information of this type, but these data are difficult to obtain and are not readily computerized in a manner that will ensure comparability.

A more fundamental difficulty with these follow-up investigations is that they are not random but targeted, so that it is difficult to make unbiased judgments of relative riskiness. These investigations focus on injuries selected on the basis of three principal criteria:

1. Injuries involving products of special interest to the CPSC. This criterion creates a bias in favor of further analysis of products regulated by the CPSC or likely to be regulated by it.

2. Fatal accidents. The investigations of such accidents may not be fruitful because the victim cannot describe the accident. The advantage of analyzing fatal accidents is that these risks are most severe and impose the greatest health loss.

3. Injuries involving products covered by the Flammable Fabrics Act, which the CPSC is legally required to investigate.

Rather than a small-scale follow-up program based on such an unrepresentative sample, a sounder approach would be to incorporate some of the more pertinent information (such as a product's manufacturer) in the basic NEISS data file.

Ideally, this additional information would include some measure of the role of consumers' actions. To provide greater comparability and meaningful responses, the phrasing of the question about safety-related actions could be made appropriate to the different types of product. For an injury with a skateboard, for example, one might ask if it was being used on a steep hill or if the user was attempting a particularly difficult maneuver. To limit reporting costs, these detailed questions could be asked on a selective but random basis rather than on the present targeted basis.

Although it is unlikely that we will ever be able fully to distinguish the relative roles of products and individual actions, we should begin to recognize the risks inherent in almost all activities, irrespective of the product used, and the limits on the risk reduction we can or should achieve. Indeed, as table 14 indicates, many of the most prom-

TABLE 14
INJURIES ASSOCIATED WITH RECREATIONAL ACTIVITIES, 1981
(thousands)

Activity	Injuries
Baseball	478
Football	470
Basketball	434
Skating	225
Swimming	126
Soccer	96
Volleyball	75
Tennis, badminton, and squash	67
Wrestling	66
Fishing	64
Gymnastics	62
Hockey	50
Snow skiing	45
Horseback riding	44
Track and field	44
Water skiing	29
Dancing	26
Golf	23
Other ball sports	22
Martial arts	19
Bowling	19
Lacrosse	10
Boxing	10
Rugby	10
Total injuries	2,514

SOURCE: CPSC, *Annual Report* (1982), pp. 22ff.

inent accident categories in the NEISS system are related not to products but to activities. The 2.5 million injuries (serious enough to require hospital treatment) in recreational activities dwarf the number of injuries from products usually considered risky. With almost 1 million additional injuries involving other forms of recreational equipment, which are summarized in table 15, the link to sports of many product accidents is even more prominent. We have not banned these sports, because the risks are typically incurred voluntarily. A similar choice by consumers may be involved in many product-related accidents as well.

A final technical limitation of the NEISS data is that the hospital sample changed in 1978, and the method of classifying product involvement was also modified at that time. Since shifts of this type make interpretation of accident trends difficult, any future change should be sufficiently comprehensive to avoid repeated shifts in the data base.

Although most data collection efforts are uncontroversial, NEISS has been the subject of critical articles and calls for its abolition.[34] In a detailed critique, an official of the National Bureau of Standards, for example, indicated how the data system could be revamped to collect information pertinent to ascertaining not the risk level per se but the existence and extent of any market failure.[35] The most salient limita-

TABLE 15
INJURIES ASSOCIATED WITH RECREATIONAL EQUIPMENT, 1981
(thousands)

Equipment	Injuries
Bicycles and bicycle accessories	518
Playground equipment	165
Exercise equipment	48
Boats, motors, and accessories for recreational use only	37
Tobaggans, sleds, snow disks, and snow tubing	32
Skateboards	28
Snowmobiles	8
Trampolines	8
Billiards and pool	6
Total injuries	850

SOURCE: CPSC, *Annual Report* (1982), pp. 22ff.

tions of NEISS—the failure to distinguish use-adjusted accident probabilities and the relative contribution of the product—become translated into limitations of CPSC policies since the NEISS data provide the primary quantitative support for evaluating present and future CPSC actions. Rather than stop collecting any accident-related information, a more sensible approach would be to start to collect meaningful accident data along the lines outlined above.

Conclusion

Many of the shortcomings of the CPSC are familiar problems of design—the absence of a formal benefit-cost test, the failure to justify the need for intervention, and inadequate emphasis on information-oriented strategies. As in other agencies, a risk-based criterion is dominant, in this case "unreasonable risk." The CPSC has exacerbated the problems associated with a risk-oriented approach by focusing on total injuries instead of the probability of injury on a use-adjusted basis. Not only may the resulting policies be inefficient, they may also raise consumer risks by eliminating products and activities much safer than those that will replace them.

Even within the context of a risk-based approach, the CPSC's regulatory strategy does not seem ideal. Why, for example, should the CPSC not ban disco dancing and cheerleading—activities that are much more hazardous than many regulated products? Unless this relative emphasis is entirely capricious, the reason for intervening or not intervening must stem from some implicit assumptions about market failure and the overall merits of regulation that can best be addressed by making those concerns explicit.

Notes

1. See Consumer Product Safety Act (hereafter CPSA), esp. sec. 30.
2. See CPSA, sec. 3 (a).
3. National Safety Council, *Accident Facts* (Chicago: National Safety Council, 1982), p. 13.
4. See CPSA, sec. 2 (a).
5. Ibid.
6. For a detailed discussion of the focus of OSHA regulations, see W. Kip Viscusi, *Risk by Choice: Regulating Health and Safety in the Workplace* (Cambridge, Mass.: Harvard University Press, 1983), chap. 2.
7. See Southland Mower v. CPSC, 619 F. 2d 499 (1980).
8. See the decision of the U.S. Supreme Court in Industrial Union Department, AFL-CIO v. American Petroleum Institute, 448 U.S. 607 (1980).
9. This format is dictated by the CPSA, sec. 4 (a).

10. See U.S. Office of Management and Budget, *Budget of the United States Government* (Washington, D.C., various years); and U.S. Consumer Product Safety Commission, *Annual Report* (Washington, D.C., 1982), for data in this paragraph.

11. See CPSA, sec. 2 (b).

12. See CPSA, secs. 30 (d), 9 (c) (2) (B).

13. See various portions of CPSA, particularly secs. 7, 8, 12, 14, 15, 18.

14. See CPSA, sec. 7 (a).

15. See CPSA, sec. 8.

16. See CPSA, sec. 9 (c) (1).

17. See CPSA, sec. 9 (c) (2).

18. See CPSA, sec. 9 (f) (2) (A).

19. See CFR 1009.8. The commission's eighth criterion is that the order of the priorities should not dictate their relative importance. For the sake of clarity, I follow the order in the CFR listing.

20. Ibid.

21. Ibid.

22. *New York Times*, February 25, 1979.

23. See Regulatory Council, *Regulatory Calendar* (1980); and *Federal Register*, vol. 25, no. 251 (December 1980), pp. 85772–77.

24. See CFR 1303.2.

25. See CFR 1205.

26. See CFR 1032.

27. See CPSA, sec. 15 (a).

28. See various portions of CPSA, including secs. 16, 20, 21, 22.

29. See CPSA, sec. 23.

30. See CPSC, *Annual Report*, pt. 1 (Washington, D.C., 1981), p. 25.

31. See CPSC, *Annual Report*, pt. 2 (Washington, D.C., 1981), p. 142.

32. See CPSC, *Annual Report*, pt. 1 1981, p. 26.

33. See CPSA, sec. 5 (a).

34. One such critique is that by Nina Cornell, Roger Noll, and Barry Weingast, "Safety Regulation," in H. Owen and C. Shultze, eds., *Setting National Priorities: The Next Ten Years* (Washington D.C.: Brookings Institution, 1976), pp. 457–504.

35. See V. K. Broussalian, "Risk Measurement and Safety Standards in Consumer Products," in N. Terleckyj, ed., *Household Production and Consumption* (New York: National Bureau of Economic Research, 1976), pp. 491–524.

4
An Overview of CPSC Policies

The policies of most risk-regulation agencies consist primarily of specification standards, of which there are thousands. Analysts of these agencies may tally up the overall number of standards, count the number of pages they entail, and perhaps discuss a few of the standards; more comprehensive treatment is usually not feasible.

In contrast, the CPSC has engaged in very little rule making. One index of major regulatory initiatives is the number of proposed regulations that have received the attention of the White House regulatory oversight process. From 1974 to 1980 the Council on Wage and Price Stability filed 300 public comments for all risk-regulation agencies, with only 5 of them pertaining to CPSC actions.[1] The agencies included in this tally were the EPA, OSHA, the CPSC, the Nuclear Regulatory Commission, the Food and Drug Administration, and the National Highway Traffic Safety Administration. Only about 1 percent of the cost of major regulations proposed during that period was imposed by CPSC standards.[2]

This apparent inactivity is also borne out in a detailed analysis of CPSC regulations. These can be divided into three categories: standards (see table 16), bans (see table 17), and informational requirements (see table 18). The standards are the most voluminous, covering twenty-one products; six product groups have been banned, and three are subject to informational requirements.

Even more striking is that only seven standards have been issued under the Consumer Product Safety Act. The majority of standards have been issued under acts inherited by the CPSC; as many have been issued under the Federal Hazardous Substances Act and under the Flammable Fabrics Act as under the CPSC's enabling legislation.

The nature of the regulations is of particular interest in view of both the Consumer Product Safety Act's explicit advocacy of performance-oriented standards and the legislative provisions for considering benefits and costs, which go beyond the narrower mandates of other agencies in their recognition of the economic aspects of regulation. Notwithstanding this directive, most of the standards and bans have

TABLE 16
SUMMARY OF CPSC STANDARDS

Product Description	Nature of Standard
Architectural glazing materials (1201)	Impact and environmental test requirements
Matchbooks (1202)	Matchbook design requirements
Walk-behind power lawn mowers (1205)	Labeling and performance requirements
Swimming pool slides (1207)	Label and specification requirements
Cellulose insulation (1209)	Flame resistance and corrosiveness test requirements
Oxygen depletion shutoff systems for unvented gas-fired space heaters (1212)	Shutoff system requirement
Toy ingestion and choking (1501)	Size tests
Electrical toys (1505)	Design and construction
Full-size baby cribs (1508)	Specification requirements
Non-full-size baby cribs (1509)	Specification requirements
Rattles (1511)	Specification requirements
Bicycles (1512)	Specification requirements
Clothing textile (1610)	Flammability test
Vinyl plastic film (1611)	Flammability test
Children's sleepwear (1615, 1616)	Flammability test
Carpets and rugs (1630)	Flammability test
Small carpets and rugs (1631)	Flammability test
Mattresses (1632)	Flammability test
Poison prevention packaging (1700)	Opening tests
Refrigerators (1750)	Door-opening test
Citizens' band antennas (1204)	Specification requirements

SOURCE: *U.S. Code of Federal Regulations*, Title 16, numbers as given in parentheses.

been based on risk criteria more than on benefit-cost trade-offs and have followed the relatively conventional specification approach—requirements for the design of matchbooks, stipulations regarding the precise spacing of crib bars, and the like. The flammability standards are the principal exception—they all include flammability testing requirements. Reliance on a testing requirement permits the CPSC to regulate consistently a wide variety of carpet materials.

Some of the CPSC's performance-oriented standards may im-

TABLE 17
SUMMARY OF CPSC BANS

Product Description	Nature of Ban
Unstable refuse bins (1301)	Stability test
Extremely flammable contact adhesives (1302)	Adhesives failing test requirements or specifications
Lead-containing paint (1303)	Specification requirement
Patching compounds with asbestos (1304)	Specification requirement
Artificial emberizing materials with asbestos (1305)	Specification requirement
Fireworks (1507)	Standard for triggering ban

SOURCE: *U.S. Code of Federal Regulations*, Title 16, numbers as given in parentheses.

pose stringent engineering requirements, however. The lawn mower standard, for example, imposes foot-probe requirements for specific probe angles, requires the use of a blade control system producing cutoff within 3.0 seconds unless the user maintains contact with the handle, and requires a specifically designed and placed "Danger" sign (that is, size, shape, and colors specified).[3] These stipulations are not tantamount to specific lawn mower designs, but they are quite different from a general performance-oriented exhortation that lawn mowers be made safe.

Although the lawn mower standard has been particularly controversial, other CPSC standards may impose even greater design requirements, not all of which are precise engineering specifications but the net effect of which is to direct firms to make specific design

TABLE 18
SUMMARY OF CPSC INFORMATIONAL REQUIREMENTS

Product Description	Nature of Requirement
Products containing chlorofluorocarbons (1401)	Performance data
Citizens' band and television antennas (1402)	Notification of hazards
Cellulose insulation (1404)	Notification of hazards

SOURCE: *U.S. Code of Federal Regulations*, Title 16, numbers as given in parentheses.

changes rather than simply to make their products safer. These requirements are best illustrated by the CPSC bicycle standard, which takes up twenty-four pages in the *Code of Federal Regulations*.[4] The CPSC mandates a variety of bicycle characteristics: an absence of sharp edges, the width of control cables (no greater than 1/4 inch), the thickness of cable clamps (no greater than 3/16 inch), the maximum distance between the brake hand lever and the handlebar grips, the maximum braking distance, the presence and placement of reflectors, and the like. Not all of these requirements appear to be strongly related to bicycle safety. These standards are a modified version of the regulations initially proposed to the CPSC by the domestic bicycle industry as a means of shutting off competition from many less expensive imports that did not meet these requirements.[5]

All bicycles complying with these requirements must be labeled with the statement "Meets U.S. Consumer Product Safety Commission Regulations for Bicycles," and this label must be "at least 6.4 cm (2.5 in.) by 17.8 cm (7 in.) setting forth the required labeling statement legibly and conspicuously in capital letters at least 0.6 cm (0.25 in.) high."[6] The effect of this label is unclear. Will bicycle riders, after having been assured of their bicycles' safety, ride faster and actually expose themselves to greater risk?

The bicycle standard is typical of CPSC standards in several respects. It includes many performance requirements, a wide variety of specification requirements, and a labeling requirement. A central difficulty with this and other multifaceted standards is that the incremental effect on safety of some of its components may be negligible. If foot probe guards are installed on lawn mowers, for example, will safety be enhanced much more by adding a cutoff device to the handle?

The labeling requirements of standards often differ—warning consumers of risks with lawn mowers and promising safety for bicycles. There is little evidence that the purpose or effectiveness of these labels has been fully analyzed or that informational alternatives to regulatory standards have been considered.

Labels have played more than a subsidiary role in CPSC regulations in cases where standards or bans are clearly not sensible. One cannot, for example, protect consumers from risks of electrocution associated with television or citizens' band antennas without banning the antennas or insulating them in a manner that would destroy their usefulness. The CPSC is, however, exploring various insulation options, an effort that seems to be a clear misallocation of the agency's resources. The informational requirement for chlorofluorocarbons is designed to keep the CPSC informed of their properties for possible future regulatory action. The final informational regulation is for cellulose insulation, which imposes a fire hazard only if it is not installed properly.

Information-oriented strategies have been undertaken almost as an afterthought, although the CPSC's discussion of informational alternatives seems to have increased under the Reagan administration. In 1983 the CPSC budgeted $250,000 to make consumers aware of the safety benefits of smoke detectors. Such advertising campaigns do not provide much new information but are intended to persuade consumers to purchase products with which they are already familiar. Such "information" efforts are much less effective than policies designed to make consumers aware of risks or safety precautions that they do not understand. The CPSC's reason for not placing greater emphasis on the information-oriented approach in its discussion of its ban of flammable contact adhesives was that "in spite of the cautionary labeling, accidents have continued to occur."[7] Imposing a no-risk requirement on alternatives to bans is clearly an impossible and unreasonable test. More generally, there was no discussion of informational alternatives that might be more effective than the present warnings or of why the existence of accidents per se serves as a justification for banning the product.

In its regulations, the CPSC has not emphasized the promotion of consumer education or performance-oriented standards. Although it has issued few regulations, those that it has promulgated have generally followed the familiar specification-standard mode.

Imminent Hazard Actions, Recalls, and Corrective Actions

In addition to issuing regulations, the CPSC takes various substantive actions against hazardous products. As noted in chapter 3, it can obtain injunctions against manufacturers of products posing imminent hazards. One might think that this regulatory mechanism was ideally suited to prompt and conclusive actions against hazardous products. In fact, the opposite is the case; these actions can be time consuming and are consequently little used.

In 1977 the CPSC brought action against manufacturers of aluminum branch circuit wiring, which has led to years of legal conflicts. The CPSC initiated the action in the U.S. district court in Washington, D.C., against twenty-six aluminum manufacturers on the grounds that their aluminum wire created an imminent fire hazard. The Anaconda Company appealed the unfavorable decision on the grounds that residential circuit branch wiring is not a consumer product within the CPSC's jurisdiction. In 1979 the U.S. court of appeals remanded the case to the district court to determine whether or not the CPSC had made the appropriate jurisdictional finding. Oral arguments were heard in 1981, and the final decision against the CPSC did not come until 1983.

A less cumbersome policy tool is the recall and corrective action authority against regulated products. During FY 1980 the CPSC issued 456 recalls of this type, but this number substantially overstates the extent of the regulatory activity since each product-manufacturer combination constitutes a separate recall. Almost two-thirds of the CPSC recalls, for example, were for various kinds of refuse bins.[8]

Much more dramatic is the extent of the recall efforts under the CPSC's section 15 authority for unregulated products and for products covered by existing regulations. In FY 1980 alone the CPSC undertook 132 separate actions against 23 million products not covered by specific standards.[9] The range of products covered is much more diverse than the refuse bin/architectual glazing/children's sleepwear pattern of recalls for regulated products. The CPSC took recall action in FY 1980 against asbestos-containing hair dryers, portable mesh cribs, rotary paint strippers, infant toys with elastic strings, indoor gym houses, roller skates, garden sprayers, toy blowguns, miter saws, night lights, portable electric drills, motorcycles, snowmobiles, and a wide range of other products.[10] The FY 1981 list is equally diverse, including toy shotguns, scuba-diving equipment, thermostats, electric player pianos, and liquid fuel containers.

One attractive feature of recalls is that they focus on clear-cut hazards. Indeed, regulating known risks rather than product characteristics might be viewed as the ultimate performance-oriented policy. The difficulty with this ad hoc approach is that, in the case of recalls of products not explicitly regulated, companies have no firm basis on which to make their investment decisions or to choose their set of products. The section 15 language indicates only that products will be viewed as posing a "substantial product hazard" if they violate an existing CPSC rule or if "a product defect . . . creates a substantial risk of injury to the public."[11] Defining a "substantial product hazard" as a defect posing a "substantial risk" is, at best, somewhat circular.

Although Congress's legislative directive is not particularly instructive, business can use past CPSC actions as an implicit statement of more detailed section 15 criteria. The difficulty with such a method is that ad hoc actions convey rather narrow principles that are restricted to the particular product. The section 15 action against leaking Coleman fuel cans suggests that leaking gasoline cans would also be subject to a recall, but it has no implications outside the specific product group.

This restrictive approach creates difficulties for businessmen since the CPSC has given them no firm indication of the performance criteria that must be met or the basis on which the CPSC will take recall actions. They are consequently placed in an uncertain environment that undermines long-run product development. Such a regulatory environment can justifiably be viewed as capricious. This shortcoming is not simply a question of equity; compliance costs and the efficiency loss to the economy will be much greater if companies are informed after the fact of the unacceptability of their product.

The CPSC has shown little awareness of the costs stemming from the uncertain environment created by recalls because its overriding concern is administrative simplicity. The reasons for reliance on this broad recall authority and "decreased use of restrictive regulatory techniques such as mandatory bans and standards" [12] are discussed quite explicitly in the CPSC's FY 1980 annual report: "While developing a mandatory standard can take years and cost hundreds of thousands of dollars, implementing a Section 15 action can, if need be, occur within weeks." [13] In effect, *the CPSC has used its section 15 authority to sidestep the checks that the rule-making process imposes on regulatory activity.* The costs to the CPSC of this regulatory mechanism are low even though the costs imposed on the private sector may be high.

These administrative procedures were designed not to harass regulatory agencies but to promote sound regulatory policies. Although other agencies would no doubt also like the leeway to regulate at will all "substantial hazards" as long as they find their regulations "in the public interest," they do not usually have such discretion. The only major analogue of this authority is the National Highway Traffic Safety Administration's recall authority for automobiles, which is narrower in scope than the CPSC's powers.

Although the CPSC claims that it should not delay in regulating hazards faced by consumers, this argument is no more persuasive for the CPSC than it is for other agencies, such as OSHA, that lack such authority. Moreover, the CPSC has quite explicit authority to deal with "imminent hazards." Although this mechanism may be time consuming, particularly when the CPSC's legal authority is in question, any shortcomings in dealing with immediate risks are better addressed by changing the imminent hazard provisions. One difference of imminent hazard actions is that the CPSC may also "initiate a proceeding to promulgate a consumer product safety rule applicable to the consumer product with respect to which such action is filed." [14]

Even without section 15 authority the CPSC need not address all hazards through ad hoc regulations. An approach intermediate between open-ended section 15 actions and a very restrictive product-specific standard is to promulgate generic standards that delineate quite precisely the kinds of criteria that will be applied and the nature of the risks that will be considered.

The OSHA carcinogen policy is a prominent example of this approach, in which the agency did not specify the particular hazards to be regulated. Rather it indicated the types of evidence of carcinogenicity that would be used and the required strength of the evidence before specific policy actions would be taken. Although the OSHA cancer policy criteria are by no means ideal, attempting to delineate the underpinnings of what will be a far-ranging policy would be a significant improvement over the section 15 approach.

Voluntary Standards

In addition to CPSC regulations and recalls, the commission also engages in activities related to voluntary standards. During FY 1980 the CPSC monitored thirty voluntary standards and participated in four.[15] Its participation entails review of draft standards and attendance at meetings, but its monitoring does not entail the commitment of CPSC resources. Though originally envisioned as a complement to CPSC standards, voluntary standards may in fact substitute for mandatory standards. The present voluntary standards for furniture upholstery flammability instituted by the Upholstered Furniture Action Council (UFAC) have forestalled CPSC regulations, which potentially could be more stringent.

Although voluntary standards are being widely embraced as a means of overcoming the antibusiness bias of regulatory agencies and drawing on the expertise of an industry, they are not always desirable. As an integral part of the decision to participate in such efforts, the CPSC should prepare economic analyses of the voluntary standards much as it does for mandatory standards. At present the CPSC attempts only partial economic analyses for selected voluntary standards. Many such standards receive no formal economic analysis.

Among the key issues to be considered with respect to voluntary standards are the following. First, what effect does the threat of intervention by the CPSC have on the informational content of the standards? Ideally, a standard should enable consumers to draw distinctions among products of differing safety, with products meeting the standard being viewed as of higher quality. If all firms subscribe to the "voluntary" standard to avoid CPSC regulation, the informational role will be dissipated, and the range of consumer choice will be narrowed in much the same way as under a mandatory standard. Second, will the voluntary standard unduly restrict the variety of products or the extent of competition in the industry? This question is best addressed by assessing the self-interest of the advocates of the voluntary approach. If the primary economic effect of a voluntary standard is to drive smaller firms out of the market or to eliminate cheaper products of lower quality, the wisdom of the voluntary approach is doubtful. Finally, there is the overriding issue of what the CPSC's involvement in a voluntary standard conveys to the consumer, which I discuss below.

General Characteristics of CPSC Policies

Conspicuously absent from all these efforts has been a valid justification of the rationale for intervention. The existence of any hazard, however small, can serve as the trigger for CPSC regulation.

There are, however, dominant patterns in CPSC regulations that provide some basis for inferring additional, often unstated, rationales for intervention. A considerable emphasis has been placed on hazards posing risks to children—toys, cribs, sleepwear, swimming pool slides, bicycles, rattles, pacifiers, roller skates, and so on. Although parents may make systematic assessments of the risks posed by the products they buy for their children, the parents are not the users and thus do not get direct feedback on the products' performance. Moreover, children who play with toys in day-care centers and elsewhere outside the home are not using toys inspected by their parents. More than for other consumer groups, a convincing case could be made regarding products for children that the buyers and the users cannot always properly assess the risks and undertake the appropriate safety-enhancing actions.

This limitation does not, however, justify all possible forms of regulation affecting children. The ill-conceived swimming pool slide standard, the voluminous bicycle standards, and the endless stream of toy regulations should be considered on their merits, just as standards for other goods are. Product variety is valued in products for children as well, and CPSC regulations no doubt have contributed to a substantial narrowing of choice.

Although the economic rationale for the CPSC's actions is often unclear, the character of its policies is not. The dominant regulatory mode has consisted of recalls and corrective actions for unregulated products. By using the broad discretion Congress gave it, the CPSC has been able to evade the rule-making process. Through its status as an independent regulatory commission, it also avoids the scrutiny of the White House regulatory oversight process. Both of these exemptions should be eliminated.

An especially controversial CPSC activity is in an area in which the CPSC has done very little—chronic hazards, such as carcinogenic risks or long-term exposures that lead to genetic damage. Although the CPSC has required asbestos-containing hair dryers to be modified, much of its chronic hazard work remains in the study phase. It is now analyzing indoor air pollution, formaldehyde, benzidine, and other hazards.

The principal issue is one of jurisdiction. Would this authority be better exercised by the EPA? The case for the EPA's involvement cannot be made on the basis that the EPA is more effective because the relative performance of the CPSC and the EPA is not at all clear and may change in the future. The primary advantage of regulation by the EPA is that the EPA has more experience in assessing the scientific basis for regulation and, if there are important synergistic effects with other air pollutants, can select which pollutants can be regulated most efficiently. Such fine-tuning rarely occurs. Moreover, the institutional barriers to providing the CPSC with proper scientific support from the EPA are not insurmountable. Perhaps the primary reason why some observers have advocated shifting authority over chronic hazards to the EPA is to diminish the role of the CPSC.

The fundamental basis for selecting the agency to have authority over chronic product hazards should be how we want to pose the policy choice. At the EPA the policy question should be how the policies affect the environment, whereas at the CPSC the policy choice should be to promote the product mix consumers would prefer if they were fully cognizant of the risks. If benefit-cost criteria were properly applied, the policy outcome should be the same at each agency. From a practical standpoint, the parochial interests of the agency are usually decisive. Ideally, the CPSC should have a firm grasp of the implications of its regulations for consumers' product choices and for the structure of the product market, whereas the EPA's primary area of expertise is how hazards affect our overall environment. To the extent that most risks specific to products do not have far-reaching implications, the CPSC's greater emphasis on product market implications may make it a more appropriate administrator of this type of regulation. Broader risks with possible synergistic effects might best be addressed by the EPA. Most product-related risks are sufficiently narrow that the CPSC will typically be the more appropriate regulatory agency.

As part of its regulatory effort the CPSC should make—but thus far has not made—systematic comparisons of product safety and chronic hazard regulations to ensure equal stringency of regulations for different types of hazards (that is, equalization of the marginal costs per health improvement). Chronic hazard regulations should produce the same health benefits per unit of cost imposed on society as other types of product safety regulations. Cost-effectiveness comparisons of this kind can best be addressed if the authority over product safety is not scattered through the government. A central agency such as the OMB should then ensure efficiency among agencies.

Another area in which the agency does very little but should do more is the provision of safety information. The CPSC does little more than require an occasional hazard warning to accompany a standard or a label, identifying products as having met CPSC standards. All manufacturers of regulated products must issue labels simply certifying their products' conformance with CPSC standards.[16] Such statements are of little use to consumers. To the extent that they are used at all, they may convey a false sense of security. CPSC standards do not guarantee that a product is risk free, and it makes little sense to lead consumers to believe that they risk no adverse consequences if they reduce the care with which they use it. In addition, CPSC standards impose different degrees of safety on different products, so that a certification of compliance does not have comparable implications for different products.

The informational content of CPSC actions is consequently very low. In some instances, such as labels testifying to the CPSC's endorsement of products' safety, the information may even be misleading and counterproductive.

A more desirable labeling system would be not to give blanket safety approval to products but to distinguish relative degrees of riskiness and the need to exercise different degrees of care. The primary objective of product safety information should not be to proclaim that certain products are safe but to inform consumers of the risks associated with different choices of products and actions so that they can choose the combinations they prefer. As I suggest in the concluding chapter, a more vigorous information-oriented strategy should supplant the more intrusive forms of intervention.

The Problem of Regulatory Uncertainty

Whenever health and safety risks are addressed whose implications are not fully understood, a regulation may be imposed that will be viewed as undesirable once better information about the risk is acquired. If firms' investments could be altered costlessly in response to changes in the regulation, the optimal approach to policy design would be simple. At any time we should base regulations on the available information and ignore the possibility that at some future date we might learn that the regulations were too stringent or too lenient.

When firms must make irreversible commitments in response to a regulation, such as an investment in redesigning a product line, repeated shifts in regulatory policy may impose severe losses. For such situations of regulatory uncertainty, I have shown that it is always desirable to underregulate whenever there is a nonzero probability that it may be desirable to relax the regulation in the future.[17] The main reason for this bias is that if it is learned that a hazard does not in fact warrant regulation, perhaps because it was originally overestimated, firms would have made needless irreversible investments in attempting to comply with the regulation. As a result, government regulators should exercise greater caution when regulating risks for which the desirability of regulation may change in the future. Rather than erring on the side of overregulation, as the CPSC and other agencies generally do, risk-regulation agencies should be more cautious.

A particularly prominent example of such regulatory uncertainty concerned firms' use of the flame-retardant Tris to comply with the children's sleepwear standards now administered by the CPSC. After it was learned that Tris was potentially carcinogenic, the sale of Tris-coated sleepwear was banned, imposing substantial losses on the textile industry. Since firms believed that these losses arose solely as a result of the government regulation, they sought compensation. Although President Carter vetoed the first bill that provided such reimbursement, at the end of 1982 President Reagan signed into law a measure that will enable these companies to seek more than $50 million in reimbursement from the federal government. This bailout decision has provoked as much controversy as the initial regulatory policy.

The difficulty arose in part from the product defect mentality that has governed our approach to product safety. If children's sleepwear burns, the obvious solution is to make it fire resistant. The technological solution that inevitably follows from the imposition of flammability standards will in turn impose new kinds of risks, as new chemical treatments and new fabrics are developed. In such a situation of uncertainty, policy makers—in this case, the Congress—should be much more prudent in their policy designs.

By paying textile firms compensation, government officials may become more cognizant of the losses that may be imposed by their actions. To the extent that the reimbursement provides such a reminder, it may lead to sounder policies in the future.

If we ignore the instructional value of the reimbursement, the issue becomes less clear. Companies were not required to use Tris to meet the performance standard but could have used other chemicals or less flammable fabrics, as some firms did. There was, however, no reason to believe that Tris was harmful, and it enabled firms to use more comfortable sleepwear materials.

Although textile firms had no additional information about the implications of Tris, the chemical producers presumably had more knowledge of the chemical and were in a better position to test its implications. Such tests are costly and time consuming, as the experience with drug regulations has demonstrated.[18] Awaiting the outcome of these tests would have led either to deferral of the compliance date or to use of an alternative, less desirable mode of compliance.

When viewed as a one-time policy, the reimbursement measure raises no efficiency issues. All Tris-related expenditures are sunk costs, so there will be no efficiency loss from reimbursing firms for their losses. As a more general policy, reimbursement for such losses may remove firms' incentive to pick the most desirable means of compliance when faced with a performance standard. Particularly in situations of differential information, where some companies may have access to superior technological knowledge, it is important to structure their incentives so that their financial interest in exploiting this knowledge is enhanced.

It is, however, desirable for policy makers to recognize the costs of mistaken government decisions. In theory, this can be done without reimbursement, although the practical significance of a liability system for bad decisions would no doubt be much more effective. Reimbursement systems for mistaken policies would also be extremely costly.

Even from the standpoint of equity, it is not obvious that the government should reimburse the textile manufacturers. There are winners and losers from most government policies, and attempts at equitable compensation are relatively minimal. There is always the chance that a policy will be viewed as unwise in the future—whether it be the Vietnam War or swine flu vaccinations—and to reimburse all who have suffered losses is usually not feasible. Rather than establish an imperfect reimbursement system, a preferable alternative would be to develop regulatory policy on a sounder basis, whereby policy makers take into account the costs imposed on firms as a result of shifts in regulatory policy. In situations in which the desirability of the regulation is speculative, it will be desirable to pursue less stringent regulations than if the basis for regulation were sound.

Notes

1. See W. Kip Viscusi, *Risk by Choice: Regulating Health and Safety in the Workplace* (Cambridge, Mass.: Harvard University Press, 1983), chap. 8, for a more comprehensive tally.

2. Ibid.

3. See CFR 1205.

4. See CFR 1512.

5. See Nina Cornell, Roger Noll, and Barry Weingast, "Safety Regulation," in H. Owen and C. Schultze, eds., *Setting National Priorities: The Next Ten Years* (Washington, D.C.: Brookings Institution, 1976), pp. 457–504, for a discussion of this incident in greater detail.

6. See CFR 1512.19.

7. See CFR 1302.5.

8. The recall data are from U.S. Consumer Product Safety Commission (CPSC), *Annual Report*, pt. 2 (Washington, D.C., 1981), pp. 73–137.

9. See CPSC, *Annual Report*, pt. 1 (Washington, D.C., 1981), p. 25.

10. See CPSC, *Annual Report*, pt. 2 (1981), pp. 45–72, for a complete list.

11. Consumer Product Safety Act (CPSA), sec. 15 (a) (2).

12. The decreased reliance on standards is noted in CPSC, *Annual Report*, pt. 2 (1981), p. 212.

13. Ibid., p. 214.

14. See CPSA, sec. 12.

15. See CPSC, *Annual Report*, pt. 2 (1981), p. 44, for a list of these efforts.

16. See CPSA, sec. 14 (a) (1).

17. This model is developed in Viscusi, *Risk by Choice*.

18. For a discussion of risk-regulation, see Henry Grabowski and John Vernon, *The Regulation of Pharmaceuticals* (Washington, D.C.: American Enterprise Institute, 1983).

5

The Effect on Product Safety

Some regulations, such as those pertaining to job safety, are so ineffectively designed and enforced that no significant improvement in safety can be identified. But weakness of the enforcement effort should not be an impediment to the CPSC's effectiveness. The widespread compliance with the CPSC's bans and standards clearly alters many characteristics of products. Unless those characteristics are unrelated to safety or consumers alter their behavior or their purchases, the regulations should enhance safety.[1]

In the extreme case of a product ban, injuries from the product will necessarily decline because the product will be used less often. Alterations in safety characteristics of products may have a similar effect. In each situation, however, consumers may substitute other products, so that their overall exposure to risk does not improve.

In this chapter I review the available evidence on trends in product safety to ascertain whether there has been any shift in product safety overall or for several prominent targets of CPSC actions. A precise assessment is prevented largely by the shortcomings of the information. The CPSC's NEISS data are not use adjusted, so that differences in risk as opposed to changes in the amount of use of a product are difficult to distinguish. In addition, the effect of recent CPSC regulations is often difficult to determine because for many consumer durables the percentage of products affected by the regulation will continue to be small until the preregulation stock of the good is replaced. These limitations contribute to the inconclusiveness of some of the risk patterns discussed in this chapter.

Accident Trends

The most meaningful test of the effect of the CPSC is an assessment of its overall effect on product safety. This approach includes the effect of substitution for goods that have been banned or modified in response to CPSC rules.

Since the CPSC's NEISS data are not aggregated for all product categories and are not available for the period before the CPSC's existence, my focus is on home accident data gathered by the National Safety Council (NSC). Table 19 summarizes the pattern of deaths from home accidents over the past two decades. The five-year changes in the accident rates, which appear in the final column, are the most meaningful since they are least sensitive to random year-to-year fluctuations.

It is essential to begin the analysis before the advent of the CPSC in 1973 because accidents have been declining throughout this century.[2] As society has become richer and less willing to incur risks, consumers have selected safer products, safer jobs, and less hazardous activities of other kinds. Indeed, the ratio of home accident rates to job accident rates has been almost invariant over the past few decades. Although the home accident rate is almost double the work accident rate, the age composition of those at home is tilted toward a higher-risk group.[3]

Accident statistics after the advent of the CPSC show a substantial decrease in accidents, as the data in table 19 indicate. But this decline is primarily a continuation of previous trends rather than a sharp departure. The establishment of the CPSC in 1973 had little apparent effect, as the data on changes in accident rates in the final

TABLE 19
HOME ACCIDENTS, 1960–1981

Year	Home Accident Death Rate	Change from Previous Year	Five-Year Change
1960	15.6	0.3	−1.7
1970	13.2	−0.5	−1.5
1971	12.9	−0.3	−2.2
1972	12.7	−0.2	−2.0
1973	12.6	−0.1	−1.4
1974	12.3	−0.3	−1.4
1975	11.7	−0.6	−1.5
1976	11.2	−0.5	−1.7
1977	10.7	−0.5	−2.0
1978	10.4	−0.3	−2.2
1979	10.0	−0.4	−2.3
1980	10.1	0.1	−1.6
1981	9.2	−0.9	−2.0

SOURCES: National Safety Council, *Accident Facts* (Chicago: National Safety Council, 1981), p. 13; and calculations by the author.

two columns indicate. If anything, a slight dampening of the deceleration in home accidents occurred immediately after the establishment of the CPSC.

Although the rate of home accidents declined more sharply in the late 1970s, this pattern was disrupted in 1980. Overall the trends are not unlike those at the beginning of the decade. The diverse elements contributing to accident trends should make one cautious in concluding that a shift in the short-term accident pattern implies that a long-term shift in accident rates has occurred. An especially important determinant of these fluctuations is the decline in the high-risk population of young children. Declines in accident rates per person may be misleading since the composition of the population has been undergoing a dramatic shift, the result being changes in safety attributable in part to changes in accident-related behavior.

The most we can conclude from overall accident trends is that home accidents do not appear to have undergone a sharp departure from their earlier trend. A similar conclusion emerges from more formal statistical analysis. Even when the age structure of the population is taken into account, there is no evidence that CPSC regulations have had a statistically significant effect on overall accident trends.[4] This does not mean that the CPSC has had no effect, only that whatever effect it may have had is so small that one cannot be confident that it differs from zero.

The Mattress Flammability Standard

The only published analysis of the CPSC that includes formal statistical tests for its effect is that by Peter Linneman.[5] His analysis considered the effect of the 1973 mattress flammability standard. Using data from the National Institute of Burn Medicine, Linneman was unable to find any significant shift in the number of burns caused by mattresses in the 1974–1977 period since the 1965–1973 period before the standard.

The absence of any statistically significant result is suggestive of the CPSC's lack of effect on safety, but it is not conclusive because the data now available do not permit precise judgments.[6] In many respects the problem is identical with that of interpreting overall accident trends. Although we can be confident that there has been no major shift in accident rates, available data are not sufficiently refined to enable us to distinguish possible small effects of the regulation.

In particular, the shift term reflecting the introduction of the standard in Linneman's analysis shows a quite substantial drop in burns from 1974 to 1977, but this coefficient is smaller than its standard error. Whether there is no effect of the standard or whether the data are simply not rich enough to estimate the effect is unclear. Since some of the equations reported by Linneman include no statistically significant coefficients of any kind, one should be somewhat cautious in drawing a precise policy conclusion from results that may be due in part to the lack of richness of the data set.

In addition, as in any assessment of the CPSC, including those in my study, the study focuses on risks from the overall use of a product, not on the risk from that product modified in response to the regulation. Since most consumers did not buy new mattresses from 1974 to 1977, the full effect of the standard will not become apparent until much later. Nevertheless, if the standard had a major effect, Linneman's analysis should have identified it.

During the period that Linneman considered, there may have been an effect of the standard that he did not capture. CPSC officials maintain that Linneman's analysis was only partial in scope since it focused only on victims of burns, whereas most fire-related mattress deaths are from smoke inhalation.[7] If the standard is effective, however, both categories of accidents should reflect some effect of the regulation.

To investigate the possibility that deaths from smoke inhalation declined, we can extend both the sample period and the types of accidents considered. In table 20 I present NSC data on trends in deaths from fire and burns and CPSC statistics on deaths from mattress and bedding fires and on overall fire-related deaths. The Linneman analysis was an obvious matter of concern to the CPSC, and the last two columns in the table constitute the CPSC's statistical defense of its effectiveness.[8]

Mattress and bedding deaths declined by 27 percent over the 1974–1978 period while fire-related deaths declined by 7 percent. The CPSC series somewhat overstates the overall rate of decline in deaths from home fires and burns, which was 2 percent from 1974 to 1977. Nevertheless, it is clear that the mattress and bedding deaths did drop by more than overall fire-related deaths. If the overall death trend reflects the trend that mattress and bedding deaths would have exhibited in the absence of the standard, as the CPSC assumes, then the conclusion might be that the standard affected the trend.

This evidence is not as clear as the CPSC suggests, however, since the size of the mattress/bedding sample is not large and the patterns are therefore very irregular.[9] The decline in death rates between 1974 and 1977 was only 12 percent. Since the data were generated from

TABLE 20
FIRE-RELATED DEATHS, 1960–1981

Year	Deaths from Home Fires and Burns (NSC)	Fire-Related Deaths from Mattresses/Bedding (CPSC)	Fire-Related Deaths (CPSC)
1960	6,350	—	—
1965	6,100	—	—
1970	5,600	—	—
1973	5,300	—	—
1974	5,100	233	1,385
1975	5,000	220	1,361
1976	5,200	185	1,418
1977	5,000	205	1,374
1978	5,100	171	1,290
1979	4,700	—	—
1980	4,400	—	—
1981	4,000	—	—

NOTE: The CPSC issued standards for mattress flammability in 1973 that became effective in 1974.
SOURCES: Data in column 1 from the National Safety Council, *Accident Facts* (Chicago: National Safety Council, 1981), p. 84, and *Accident Facts* (Chicago: National Safety Council, 1982). Data in columns 2 and 3 from CPSC, *Annual Report*, pt. 2 (Washington, D.C., 1981), p. 261, based on CPSC death certificates.

fragmentary reports and the sample size and the states reporting data changed from year to year, it is not possible to ascertain whether the low number of deaths in 1976 and 1978 reflects especially safe mattresses or is attributable to the sample in those years.

If the CPSC standard is effective, the overall trend in deaths from home fires should also show the effect of the standard. There is no readily apparent downward shift in total fire-related deaths or the fire-related death rate. Both continued to drop at their prestandard rate of decline. The evidence on total fire-related deaths provides no solid support for dismissing the negative conclusions of the Linneman analysis.

Although the evidence is sufficiently clear to conclude that the standard has not had a major effect, it could have had some effect that we are unable to estimate reliably because it is not large. The appropriate matter for policy evaluation is the magnitude of the effect and the extent to which the benefits, if any, exceed the costs.

Child-resistant Bottle Caps

The standard that most CPSC officials hail as the CPSC's greatest success is the requirement that bottle caps for aspirin and other dangerous drugs and substances be child resistant. These regulations were the result of the Poison Prevention Packaging Act of 1970, which was enacted several years before the CPSC was established. The first wave of implementation took several years and included action by the FDA against five substances in 1972–1973 and CPSC requirements for six substances in 1973–1974. The initial targets for regulation included aspirin, illuminating and kindling preparations, and prescription drugs. The CPSC broadened its protective packaging requirements in 1977 to include iron preparations and paint solvents and in 1980 to include acetaminophen preparations.

Aspirin accounted for the greatest number of ingestions. In the year of the introduction of protective caps for aspirin, aspirin accounted for about 10 percent of all poisonings. A more informative measure of its role is that it accounted for 39 percent of all poisonings from products covered by the packaging act.[10]

The effort to prevent poisonings by aspirin began before the imposition of the protective bottle cap requirements. In the mid-1960s firms began to limit the number of tablets per bottle, to use warning labels, and to place snap caps rather than screw tops on bottles. In addition, there was a widespread consumer education campaign to limit children's access to drugs. In 1969 two leading manufacturers voluntarily introduced child-resistant caps, and in 1969–1970 aspirin poisoning rates declined. In 1972 the requirements of the Poison Prevention Control Act were applied to aspirin, and in 1973 and 1974 the poisoning rates declined, as shown in the final column of table 21. Aspirin poisoning rates followed the patterns one would expect from an effective standard, and the CPSC points to such data as evidence of its effectiveness.[11]

The key assumption underlying a conclusion that the standard was effective is that child-resistant caps were the major influence on the changes in the 1969–1974 period. There was also, however, a dramatic shift in the consumption of aspirin as sales of acetaminophen products (such as Tylenol) rose dramatically beginning in 1969. By 1980 all miscellaneous analgesics, such as acetaminophen, accounted for 53,030 poisonings. If consumers were substituting acetaminophen for aspirin products, as was indeed the case, one would expect the nonaspirin poisoning rates to rise.

Even apart from this adjustment, one would expect aspirin poisonings to have declined throughout this century wholly apart from

TABLE 21
POISONINGS, 1968–1981

Year	Poisoning Death Rate	Poisoning Death Rate (under five years of age)	Reported Aspirin and Analgesic Poisonings (under five years of age)	Aspirin and Analgesic Poisoning Rate (under five years of age)
1968	1.3	1.6	168,090	938.5
1969	1.5	1.4	160,050	920.9
1970	1.8	1.3	110,280	642.3
1971	1.8	1.4	103,850	602.4
1972	1.8	1.4	108,660	635.4
1973	1.8	1.2	87,940	521.9
1974	1.9	0.8	69,320	420.4
1975	2.2	0.7	72,920	452.4
1976	1.9	0.7	62,740	401.6
1977	1.6	0.6	59,630	383.2
1978	1.4	0.5	63,290	402.1
1979	1.3	0.5	62,180	387.1
1980	1.2	0.4	53,540	327.9
1981	1.1	0.3	—	—

NOTE: The Poison Prevention Packaging Act was passed in 1970. The FDA took action against five substances in 1972–1973; the CPSC established requirements for six substances in 1973–1974.
SOURCES: Data in columns 3 and 4 from unpublished Poison Control Center computer printouts; columns 1 and 2 from published and unpublished National Safety Council data.

CPSC regulations. The poisoning death rate (per 100,000 population) averaged 2.9 from 1913 to 1922, 2.2 from 1923 to 1932, 1.5 from 1933 to 1942, 1.2 from 1943 to 1952, and 0.9 from 1953 to 1962.[12] The death rate rose in subsequent years, in part because of the changing age structure of the population and shifts in consumption patterns (see data in table 21). I have obtained a similar result using a formal statistical analysis of poisoning rates.[13] There is no evidence of any significant downward shift in aspirin poisoning rates after the safety cap regulation. There was, however, an upward shift in analgesic poisonings, which were not subject to safety cap requirements. This combination of effects suggests that parents became more lax about access to medicines after the advent of safety caps.

There is no solid evidence that the decline in aspirin deaths departed from the pattern one would expect on the basis of long-run trends. Other regulated products follow a similar pattern.[14] What is most disturbing is that poisoning deaths from unregulated products have not dropped at the same rate as those from aspirin products. Indeed, there was a rise in both total poisonings and the poisoning death rate in the mid-1970s. The CPSC views these trends more optimistically, claiming that the relatively better performance of regulated products is a sign of protective caps' effectiveness.[15]

This explanation would be more compelling if there had been a shift in the trend of the aspirin poisoning rate. Since aspirin constitutes an increasingly small share of the pain reliever market, one would be hard pressed to argue that this hazard would have been increasing had it not been for protective caps.

A more likely alternative is that the use of protective caps has made parents more lax about their children's access to hazardous products. Since hazardous substances are presumed to be "child-proof," there is less emphasis on preventing children's access to them.

This regulation-induced neglect is consistent with actual poisoning patterns.[16] Whereas only 34 percent of all aspirin and analgesic poisonings in 1972 were from child-resistant bottles, by 1978 this figure reached 66 percent. Over two-thirds of all aspirin poisonings are from bottles protected by CPSC-mandated caps. In addition, almost half (47 percent) of all poisonings are from bottles that have been left open. Although the Poison Control Center does not gather data on the fraction of safety-capped bottles left open, the prevalence of open-bottle poisonings for analgesics (which have fewer safety caps) is almost as great as for aspirin, so that the child-resistant caps on closed bottles appear to be ineffective in a great many instances.

If parents believe that most hazardous substances are in safe, child-resistant containers, they will be more lax about their children's access to such products. For any given level of access, child-resistant packaging will reduce the risk. But as the exposure to the risk of regulated products increases, the effectiveness of the protective requirement will be at least partially offset, leading to a dampening of the regulatory effect. Similarly, the increased neglect will lead to an upsurge in poisonings from unregulated products, as compared with the trend they would have followed. Each of these patterns is consistent with available poisoning data. The rather alarming poisoning trends suggest that the reliance on technological solutions to product safety problems may be ineffective to the extent that it fails to take into account consumers' responses to the regulation.

One might also question the overall desirability of this regulation. CPSC-approved child-resistant caps are now designed so that an individual aged ten to forty-five can open the containers within five minutes. For people at the upper end of this range who open such caps once a day the total added time per year can be as much as thirty hours. If this consumer's wage rate is $10 per hour, the time cost is equivalent to a $300 annual loss. If the consumer makes choices that imply a value of his child's life of $1 million, he will prefer not to use the protective caps unless they reduce the risk of death by at least 3/10,000. Even if all poisonings were fatal—and few of them are—protective caps would have to eliminate half of all poisonings for them to justify the added time costs. If the consumer were able to open the caps within thirty seconds, protective caps would have to eliminate 5 percent of all poisonings. Since there is no evidence of any beneficial effect of safety caps on poisonings, the desirability of this regulation is questionable.

In 1983 the CPSC appeared to have recognized the importance of the inconvenience of such caps, particularly for elderly people who may require more than the five minutes that prime-age consumers have to conquer the child-resistant caps for the caps to be approved by the CPSC. Rather than simply initiating an investigation of ways to make these requirements less burdensome to the elderly, the CPSC should undertake a broader examination of the justification for the regulation. First, what is the cost of child-resistant packaging both in increased consumer time and in inconvenience? Second, how do consumers respond to the regulation in the access that they give their children to these products, and what is the net effect on safety?

Finally, are there alternatives to child-resistant packaging that are preferable? One possibility recently dismissed by the CPSC because of its lack of an absolute protective requirement was to have protective caps that could be easily disengaged by consumers who did not wish to take advantage of them. Consumers who did not have young children would then have the option of removing the caps so as to decrease the regulatory burden. Those who wished to use the caps could continue to do so. This form of regulation addresses all problems that might arise because of the fixed costs of providing protective caps to a small segment of the consumer population. The only remaining justification for a sweeping requirement is a belief that consumers are irrational and cannot make wise safety decisions. Even if this were the case—and the CPSC has never shown that it is—the CPSC must balance any benefits of overcoming this irrationality against the time impositions resulting from a general protective cap requirement. In the absence of such evidence, the optional protective cap standard for all regulated products is clearly preferable to the present mandatory version.

Crib Regulations

Along with the protective packaging requirements, the CPSC crib standards are among the most widely cited examples of CPSC success stories. The first crib standard was a 1973 regulation for full-size baby cribs.[17] This was followed by a 1976 standard for non-full-size baby cribs.[18] The intent of the standards was similar, but the standard for full-size cribs was broader in scope.

Most purchasers of cribs over the past decade are familiar with the 1973 spacing requirements for crib bars. To prevent babies' heads from becoming caught between the vertical bars, the CPSC required that the spacing not exceed 2⅜ inches. The potential efficacy of this part of the regulation is not controversial.

The regulation also affected the height of the crib, not to be under 9 inches in its lowest position or under 26 inches in its highest position. Regulating crib height options should reduce the risk that babies will fall out of cribs if parents adjust the height of the mattress properly. If the major safety problem is that parents set the mattress too high rather than that crib height options are too few, increasing the depth of the crib will not be particularly effective.

Finally, the crib standard includes other requirements pertaining to crib construction, assembly instructions, and labeling. These are less clearly related to safety. The size of cribs, for example, is precisely specified: "The interior dimensions shall be 71 ± 1.6 centimeters (28 ± ⅝ inches) wide as measured between the innermost surfaces of the crib sides and 133 ± 1.6 centimeters (52 ⅜ ± ⅝ inches) long as measured between the innermost surfaces of the crib end panels, slats, rods, or spindles."[19] As these requirements suggest, the crib standard is a comprehensive specification for crib design rather than a narrowly focused requirement for spacing of crib bars.

The net effect of this regulation is obscured by the unevenness of crib injury trends. Table 22 summarizes the trends from 1973 to 1981. To ensure comparability, all categories of crib-related injuries were pooled. Although the CPSC has separate classifications for cribs and portable cribs, most injuries are in the category "cribs, not specified." Moreover, the divisions among crib categories changed over time, and pooling was the best way to maintain consistency.

If we exclude 1981, which may reflect an aberrational increase in injuries, there appears to be a moderate drop in crib injuries. Crib injuries per 1,000 births also declined, as shown by the second column of table 22. Even this downward trend is not unexpected in view of the secular increase in safety.

In addition, there is no a priori justification for ignoring 1981. If cribs had not already been regulated extensively, an explosion in crib-related injuries such as that in 1981 would have prompted immediate action by the CPSC. To smooth out the overall trend, let us compare the average crib injury per 1,000 births from 1973 to 1976 with the analogous figure for 1978 to 1981. For each period, we obtain an identical average figure for injuries per 1,000 births of 2.84.

TABLE 22
CRIB INJURIES, 1973–1981

Year	Total Crib Injuries	Crib Injury Rate per 1,000 Births
1973	9,753	3.11
1974	9,963	3.15
1975	7,797	2.48
1976	8,333	2.63
1977	9,791	2.94
1978	9,149	2.75
1979	8,947	2.56
1980	9,331	2.59
1981	12,617	3.46

NOTE: A 1973 CPSC regulation specified spacing requirements for the vertical bars on full-size baby cribs; a 1976 regulation covered non-full-size cribs.
SOURCES: NEISS data; U.S. Bureau of the Census, Current Population Reports (Washington, D.C., 1982); and calculations by the author.

The NEISS data give no indication that the crib standards have had any favorable effect whatsoever. Whether these results are attributable to a lack of an effect on safety or to a weakness of the data is not clear. To the extent that the latter explanation is correct, it points up the shortsightedness of letting temporary swings in NEISS statistics govern CPSC policy.

In contrast to the analysis of the mattress standard, for cribs we have data over a long period of time over which to evaluate the standard's effect. Although some preregulation cribs continued to be used, the current stock of cribs in use should be largely in compliance with the CPSC standards. The absence of a marked effect on safety suggests that even products whose design is almost completely dictated by government regulation give no assurance of safety.

Swimming Pool Slides, Carpets and Rugs, and Bicycles

The difficulty in identifying a favorable effect of the CPSC on safety pertains to other standards as well. In this section I review the trends in reported injuries for several other major regulated product categories to ascertain whether there has been a shift in safety for some principal targets of CPSC actions. Since my focus is on the NEISS data, the time period considered is not very long. The unique advantage of this data base is that it provides safety information for narrowly defined product groups.

In table 23 I present national injury trends for swimming pool slides and for carpets and rugs. These national figures are based on extrapolations by the CPSC from the NEISS data. The 843 swimming pool slide injuries in 1977, for example, have been projected on the basis of 29 injury reports at hospitals in the NEISS sample. The sample size for carpets and rugs is much greater, so the patterns should be more reliable.

The swimming pool slide standard issued in January 1976 is associated with relatively few product-related injuries—under 1,000 in all but three years.[20] This small sample size makes the data a potentially unreliable index of prevailing safety. The low number of injuries has also led to substantial criticism of the CPSC for even having pursued such a standard. The notoriety of this standard stems not from its role in safety regulation but from its inconsequential nature. In *Aqua Slide 'N' Dive* v. *Consumer Product Safety Commission*, the U.S. court of appeals found that the CPSC had never determined that the standard would be effective in promoting safety.[21] Although the CPSC too has had misgivings about the desirability of the standard, in 1981 it de-

TABLE 23
INJURIES FROM SWIMMING POOL SLIDES AND FROM CARPETS AND RUGS, 1974–1981

Year	Injuries Involving Swimming Pool Slides	Injuries Involving Carpets and Rugs
1974	552	18,478
1975	852	18,108
1976	2,100	17,829
1977	843	25,661
1978	979	32,180
1979	985	35,450
1980	1,878	47,595
1981	1,937	38,587

NOTE: Effective date of swimming pool slide standard, January 1976; effective date of carpet and rug standard, December 1975.

SOURCE: CPSC, NEISS computer printouts.

cided that the cost of formally revoking it was too high to be worthwhile.

The effectiveness of the standard is certainly not borne out by the data. Injuries have risen substantially since the standard was established: average annual injuries from 1976 to 1980 were 1,357, an increase from 702 during the prestandard period, 1974–1975. The aberrationally high numbers of injuries in 1976 and 1980 suggest that the data may be too unreliable to conclude that injuries have accelerated since the standard, but there is certainly no evidence whatsoever that the standard has had a favorable effect.

Somewhat surprisingly, a similar pattern is exhibited by carpets and rugs, which are covered by CPSC flammability standards.[22] After remaining relatively stable through 1976, injuries for these products rose considerably beginning in 1977, just a little over one year after the standard was promulgated. Prestandard average annual injuries were only 18,293 in 1974 and 1975, far below the 32,884 average thereafter.

This pattern is the opposite of what one would expect for an effective standard. Although rug sales may have increased and there may have been a change in the reporting of injuries,[23] these are unlikely to be the dominant factors.[24] One possibility is that non-fire-related accidents have been increasing, notably falls on carpeted surfaces. Since there is no reason to believe that individual consumers are becoming more accident prone, a possible explanation of the accident shift is the change in the composition of carpet material. New synthetic carpet fabrics may be more slippery than materials such as wool that had a greater share of the market in earlier years. The CPSC's carpet flammability standard may have contributed to this problem since less flammable carpets designed to meet CPSC regulations may pose risks of other kinds. When regulating products with multiple risks, reducing one form of risk may lead to increases in other risks, as the CPSC learned in the Tris experience.

What is particularly disturbing is that the CPSC's Flammable Fabrics Report, which is required under the Flammable Fabrics Act and was included in its latest annual reports, never discussed any carpet or rug injury data.[25] The CPSC focused on seemingly more favorable trends, such as those for mattresses. Although much smaller escalations in risk have prompted CPSC action, in this case, in which a standard already existed, the CPSC has chosen to ignore the apparent ineffectiveness of its standard and what may even be a counterproductive effect on overall safety. The CPSC simply noted that carpets and rugs merited "continuing attention."

The final case study is the CPSC bicycle standard, which imposed extensive bicycle design requirements. The CPSC issued this standard in November 1978, so that we have three years of bicycle accident data to evaluate its effect (see table 24). Overall bicycle-related

TABLE 24
BICYCLE INJURIES, 1974–1981

Year	Bicycle Injuries	Bicycle Injuries per 1,000,000 Bicycles in Use
1974	519,952	7,064.6
1975	520,339	7,089.1
1976	503,308	6,764.9
1977	546,479	7,106.4
1978	491,930	6,355.7
1979	557,883	7,508.5
1980	503,594	7,394.9
1981	549,863	8,741.9

NOTE: The CPSC issued standards for bicycle design in November 1978.
SOURCES: Injury data based on CPSC, NEISS computer printouts; data on bicycles in use from the Bicycle Manufacturers Association of America.

injuries were highest in 1979 and 1981, with a temporary dip in 1980. Once again the NEISS data suggest a very uneven trend that provides little apparent evidence for the effectiveness of CPSC regulations.

There is little a priori reason to believe that the CPSC regulation exacerbated bicycle safety problems. A more likely explanation for the recent upsurge in accidents is that riding bicycles has become more popular as a form of recreation and as a means of transportation. To adjust for this possibility, the final column in table 24 presents a use-adjusted injury measure, the number of injuries divided by the number of bicycles in use (using the seven-year useful life assumption advocated by the Bicycle Manufacturers Association of America). Once again there is no apparent decline, and there is a marked upsurge in accident rates in 1981.

It is possible that this pattern is due to greater intensity of bicycle use, but presumably use and sales are strongly correlated. Since the seven-year moving sales average may not provide an accurate index of 1981 use, one might wish to use 1981 sales as a proxy for bicycling intensity in 1981. But 1981 bicycle sales were at their lowest since 1976; so there is little apparent upsurge in bicycle use. The main sales increase occurred between 1972 and 1974, when there was an explosion in the sales of ten-speed bicycles.

In view of the tenuous relation between the CPSC standard and bicycle safety, it is not surprising that there is little apparent effect of the standard. What is more troubling from the standpoint of using NEISS data for policy formation is that it is unlikely that these data provide a consistent and accurate portrayal of trends in bicycle accidents. The only hypothesis consistent with the data is that accidents decline temporarily in all even-numbered years. There is no apparent trend to indicate either an improvement in safety or a significant worsening of safety as a result of the regulation.

Conclusion

Neither the total accident data nor the product-specific data point to any major success by the agency. This finding is particularly surprising in as much as my analysis focused on some prominent CPSC regulations. Although some kinds of injuries have diminished, available data do not enable us to identify any favorable effects of the standards or any shifts from decreases in risk that were already occurring.

It was particularly disturbing that the patterns in the NEISS data were irregular; this difficulty was especially acute for narrowly defined product groups. The shortcomings in the data do not simply pose a problem for policy evaluation. They also affect the design of policies based on this information. The picture that emerges is one of an agency selecting policies on a risk-based criterion for which the underlying accident information is not very precise and often not meaningful. If aberrations in the data series on injury trends lead the CPSC to mount an attack on newly emerging hazards, as has happened so often in the past, the result will be a set of regulations designed to ameliorate non-existent crises. A more reliable basis for policy is to assess the sources of market failure and to address policies to those inadequacies rather than let policies be determined by the random fluctuations of data on injury rates.

Notes

1. Diminished safety-enhancing action by consumers will dampen the beneficial effects of regulations even when the net effect on safety is favorable.

2. For a much longer-term perspective on all accidents—including those at home, those at work, and overall risks—see W. Kip Viscusi, *Risk by Choice: Regulating Health and Safety in the Workplace* (Cambridge, Mass.: Harvard University Press, 1983).

3. See National Safety Council, *Accident Facts* (Chicago: National Safety Council, 1982), p. 13

4. For the National Safety Council home accident rate data from 1934 to 1981, a representative equation using a 1973–1981 dummy variable shift term for the effect of CPSC is the following:

$$\text{Home accident rate}_t = 18.98 + 0.28 \text{ home accident rate}_{t-1}$$
$$(3.24) \quad (0.10)$$
$$-0.0029 \text{ real per capita consumption}_t$$
$$+(0.0008)$$
$$-0.037 \text{ CPSC dummy variable}$$
$$+(0.643)$$
$$+\text{series of data collection shift variables}$$

Numbers in parentheses are standard errors. The $\bar{R}^2$ is .97, and the Durbin-Watson statistic is 1.81. Similar results were obtained from a postregulation simulation.

5. See CFR 1632 for the standard; Peter Linneman, "The Effects of Consumer Safety Standards: The 1973 Mattress Flammability Standard," *Journal of Law and Economics*, vol. 23 (1980), pp. 461–79, for a critique of it; U.S. Consumer Product Safety Commission (CPSC), *Annual Report*, pt. 2 (Washington, D.C., 1981); and Robert Kurtz, "Review of the Journal Article on Mattress Flammability Standards," memorandum to Walter Hobby, Consumer Product Safety Commission, 1981.

6. This shortcoming of the study reflects not a deficiency in Linneman's statistical approach but a property of the data, which Linneman also recognizes.

7. See Kurtz, "Review of Article," for supporting documentation.

8. A much more effective defense was the internal CPSC memorandum by Kurtz, "Review of Article."

9. CPSC, *Annual Report*, pt. 2 (1981).

10. This calculation used the ingestions for the base year of each substance's regulation. Data are based on unpublished CPSC figures using Poison Control Center data.

11. This information is summarized in the CPSC's fact sheet "Poison Prevention Packaging Act."

12. These data are from National Safety Council, *Accident Facts* (1982), p.18.

13. See W. Kip Viscusi, "An Assessment of the Safety Impacts of Consumer Product Safety Regulation," Duke Center for Study of Business Regulation, Working Paper No. 83-10 (1983).

14. These conclusions are based on a preliminary statistical analysis of the Poison Control Center data.

15. The CPSC sent such data on regulated products to the National Safety Council for inclusion in its *Accident Facts* (1982), p. 83.

16. The data cited below were compiled from unpublished computer printouts from the Poison Control Center.

17. See CFR 1508.

18. See CFR 1509.

19. This is an excerpt from the crib dimension requirements in CFR 1508.3.

20. See CFR 1207 for a description of this standard.

21. The details of this case are discussed in *Regulation* (May/June 1980), p. 9.

22. See CFR 1630 and 1631 for these standards.

23. As discussed in chapter 2, the NEISS data reporting system changed in 1978, which was after the upward shift in injuries in 1977.

24. CPSC, *Annual Report*, pt. 2 (1981).

25. These requirements appear in CFR 1512.

6
Benefits and Costs of CPSC Regulations

A central concern in evaluating the CPSC is the extent to which the benefits of its efforts exceed the costs. Even if the bans and standards were selected mainly on the basis of risk-based concerns, such an emphasis could be justified if these efforts were able to do so inexpensively. Such a fortunate result did not prevail, largely because of the CPSC's misdirected emphasis. As the case studies in this chapter indicate, the CPSC has provided little in the way of a valid justification for its efforts, which in turn has produced policies that on balance are not very desirable.

This evaluation of the merits of CPSC policy is necessarily prospective since the CPSC does not gather information on the actual effects of its policies. The suggestive evidence on the safety effects of these policies presented in chapter 5 sheds some light on the actual benefits of the CPSC's actions. Since the CPSC's policy analyses are typically based on very optimistic benefit assumptions, the actual policy effects are in all likelihood less favorable than the agency had anticipated.

The purpose of reviewing the CPSC's policy analyses is not to evaluate the competence of the agency's staff support; the CPSC's regulatory analyses do not much differ in quality from those prepared by other regulatory agencies before the Reagan administration imposed stringent regulatory analysis requirements on executive branch agencies. Reviewing the underlying analyses the CPSC prepared for its regulatory decisions can give additional insight into the kinds of factors emphasized in the commissioners' decision making. To offer a more comprehensive perspective, my review considers not only the preliminary regulatory analyses, which in a few instances were also reviewed in public filings of the Council on Wage and Price Stability, but also subsequent revisions in the analyses. The fundamental implication of this review is not that the policy concerns reflected in the analyses are inconsistent with the commission's legislative mandate but that they fall far short of an efficient approach to policy that would also be consistent with the CPSC's legislation.

The Matchbook Standard

One of the most controversial of the CPSC's regulations was its safety standard for matches.[1] In 1976 the CPSC proposed a safety standard for matchbooks directed primarily at reducing burns caused by matches. The original proposal included improved quality control, self-extinguishing flames, a latching device, and striking surfaces on the reverse side of the matchbook. The final standard promulgated in 1978 was somewhat more limited in its principal requirements, which included the following:

- friction on the outside back cover or the bottom of the matchbook
- ability of the matchbook to remain closed without external force
- improved quality control
- a manufacturer's label and warning sign on the box: "For safety, store in a cool, dry place"[2]

This standard created substantial controversy because it was viewed as relatively inconsequential, perhaps even frivolous, especially in the initial, more restrictive proposals. As one of the first actions taken by the newly established CPSC, it suggested that there had been little basis for creating the agency. While these doubts appear well founded, my focus here is on ascertaining whether this was a desirable standard, irrespective of whether it was a major safety-related policy.

The fundamental question never addressed by the CPSC or by the White House oversight process is, Why should we have a matchbook standard?[3] What inadequacy in the market made government intervention desirable? The properties of matches are well known, as are the risks involved in their use.

One possible basis for the standard can be inferred from the distribution of accidents with matches. Almost 13 percent of the injuries occur to children ages nine and under.[4] This age distribution is quite different from that of child-oriented products such as toys; so children's access to matches is one source of accidents but not the primary cause of accidents. Most accidents are to people who are older and who should be cognizant of the risks.

Since the CPSC gave as the first justification for issuing the rule a desire to prevent accidents to children and the mentally impaired, one wonders why it did not pursue a quite different policy.[5] Rather than worry about matters such as staples on matchbook covers, which are not aimed directly at misuse of matches, the CPSC could have assessed the merits of an informational campaign to reduce the access to matches of groups unable to use them safely. Such an informational effort might not have been particularly effective, however, since the hazards posed by matches are well known and are not due solely to access by narrowly defined population groups. The fundamental problem is not that of a defective product but that some individuals cannot be relied on to use matchbooks, lighters, or other fire-related products safely. The final CPSC rule was directed at making matchbooks safer for responsible users, not for persons who should not be permitted access to matches. The key issue is not matchbook safety but proper use of a product that is hazardous if it is misused.

The misdirected focus of the CPSC policy stems largely from a failure to analyze the accident-generating process. This omission also characterizes critiques of the CPSC's matchbook analysis, though to a somewhat lesser extent.[6] Accidents are generated by a process not unlike those involved in the production of desired goods and services. The ingredients of this process include the source of the fire (matches or lighters), other pertinent material inputs (combustibles such as gasoline or flammable fabrics), and safety-related actions of the consumer. To single out matches as the cause of fire-related injuries is not only simplistic, it leads policy makers to ignore the combination of factors that give rise to accidents. In this instance it ignores more fundamental aspects of the accident-generating process, notably the careless use of matches and access to matches by children.

The arbitrariness of isolating matches as the appropriate target for regulation can be seen by surveying the performance of other fire-related products. Although injuries related to matches now total about 7,000 annually, there are an equal number of injuries involving ash trays, 16,000 injuries related to chimneys and fireplaces, and 29,000 injuries from liquid fuels.[7] Cigarettes, lighters, combustible fabrics, and other products also contribute to fire-related accidents. Quite simply, there are many contexts in which fires are not safe, and it is not appropriate simply to blame defective products for all the adverse outcomes.

This fundamental observation has continued to be ignored by the CPSC, which is now assessing the desirability of regulating wood-burning stoves. Preliminary evidence suggests that, like accidents with matches, the accidents derive primarily not from product defects but from inadequacies in consumers' behavior, such as failure to remove the creosote buildup in chimneys.

By not focusing on the accident-generating process, the CPSC implicitly attributes most or all risks to product defects so that it can then ascribe unlimited benefits to its standards. Risks are identified, and the explicit or implicit assumption is usually that the standard will substantially eliminate them. Even when based on such boundless optimism, the attractiveness of CPSC standards is questionable. Although the total cost of the originally proposed standard was moderate (only $68 million), even with complete effectiveness it would cost $7,000 to prevent each matchbook injury. Most such injuries are minor. For more severe accidents, the cost of the standard would be $240,000 per hospitalization prevented.[8] This value is roughly an order of magnitude larger than the value workers are willing to pay to prevent the risk of a lost-workday injury, as reflected in data on wage-risk trade-offs.[9] Even if fully effective, the standard would not appear to be desirable.

In reality the matchbook standard has not made matches risk free. Between 1975 and 1980 matchbook-related accidents declined from 9,500 to 7,000.[10] Much of the decrease was no doubt due to the increased use of butane lighters and the decreased size of the high-risk population of young children. If the original standard had been assumed to lead to the actually observed one-fourth reduction of accidents, its cost would have been $28,000 per injury and $960,000 per hospitalization—both quite high. Indeed, the hospitalization cost estimate is double the value workers in high-risk jobs implicitly place on fatal accidents and roughly comparable to some estimates of the value of life for workers in more typical occupations.

It should be noted that all these calculations pertain to the entire standard. What the CPSC should do, but never does, is to assess the incremental cost-effectiveness of each component of its multipart standards.

Rather than justify the cost-effectiveness of its final standard, the CPSC noted that there were many matchbook-related accidents and that the standard would cost only a "few cents" per box of matches.[11] But seemingly trivial costs should not be imposed on consumers if the *incremental reduction in risk* is even more trivial. A danger of seemingly minor regulations is that the total effect of such undesirable efforts by all agencies may be quite consequential.

Even if the entire matchbook standard is not desirable on economic grounds, particular portions of it may be able to pass the test of economic desirability. Since the CPSC never estimated the incremental effects, data are not available to ascertain whether a streamlined version of the standard is desirable.

In the absence of a firm economic justification for any of the provisions of the matchbook standard, the CPSC could have proposed a voluntary standard whereby, for example, firms could choose whether to put the striking surface on the back of the matchbook cover. Such voluntary standards might be coupled with a more refined quality grading system than is now employed so that the agency could play a role in safety certification as well as provide the stimulus for safety-related innovations. Present CPSC safety labels are applicable to all products of a particular type—since noncomplying products cannot be sold—so that their only informational role is to indicate the average quality of the entire product group. Voluntary labels would create distinctions among products within a particular group.

The matchbook standard reflects several persistent inadequacies of the CPSC approach:

- failure to establish an inadequacy in the market and its relation to the standard
- failure to analyze the accident-generating process and alternative ways of influencing it
- discussion of the total risk, not the incremental reduction in risk
- failure to compare the incremental costs and incremental benefits

The Architectural Glazing Standard

In January 1977 the CPSC issued a safety standard for architectural glazing materials.[12] The primary risk was of cuts by glass from products such as storm doors, fixed glass panels, patio doors, and shower enclosures. In an effort to reduce such accidents, the CPSC imposed a series of performance tests that can only be met by safety glass that has been sufficiently tempered or laminated. This standard was also noteworthy in that it was the first national building standard ever proposed by the CPSC.

The CPSC followed its typical approach. It imposed stringent performance requirements for glass after providing two principal pieces of information—the number of glass-related injuries and the cost of the standard.[13] These data, though not irrelevant, do not constitute a sound basis for intervention unless one assumes, as the CPSC implicitly does, that the existence of a substantial risk is alone sufficient to justify intervention.

Although 185,000 people are injured annually in glass-related accidents, only 75,000 injuries involve products affected by the standard.[14] But even this injury estimate is not pertinent, except as an upper bound on possible effects, unless one assumes that the standard will prevent all injuries from products covered by the standard. Since the CPSC never estimated the differential effects of the standard, it never assessed its incremental benefits, which is what is pertinent to policy design.

The CPSC did estimate the incremental costs, which ranged from $45 to $62 million annually. Whether this expenditure is warranted depends on the value of the risk reduction. If the standard is 75 percent effective and injuries are worth $300, the benefits are only $5 million. [15] An injury value of $3,700 would make the standard desirable even at the upper range of the cost estimates. The injury value should be the discounted value of the reduction in accidents, many of which will occur in the distant future.

To make such judgments, we need detailed information on the distribution of the severity of accidents prevented and the timing of the accident reductions. The limited information available indicates that only 2 percent of the accidents require hospitalization and most of the others are minor lacerations. If we assume that hospitalizations have a comparable value to lost-workday job accidents, we can assign a value of $20,000 to each hospitalization, which reflects the implicit value to the accident victim, including the costs of pain and suffering. [16] The rest of the accidents, considered minor by the CPSC, will be assigned a value of $300, which overstates the medical costs. [17] The overall benefit estimate per accident is $694, when averaged over the entire group of accidents. (After appropriate discounting, this figure is even lower.) This amount is one-fifth of that needed for the standard to be warranted, assuming that the standard eliminates 75 percent of all injuries from glass products covered by the standard.

The judgment to pursue the policy is not and should not be based on the medical costs alone but rather on the estimated value of the accident reduction to the beneficiaries of the policy. What this example suggests is that simple identification of a hazardous product that can be regulated is not an appropriate basis for policy. The existence of a risk does not imply that the benefits of regulation exceed the costs.

The Power Lawn Mower Standard

Perhaps the best-known CPSC standard is that for power lawn mowers. Although the standard was issued in 1979, its provisions were phased in, so that it began to be fully effective only in 1982. [18] The development of the standard provoked so much controversy that the Congress took the highly unusual step of amending its form. Since proposed lawn mower standards had been subjected to critical reviews by the Council on Wage and Price Stability in 1975 and 1977 after the issue was originally raised by the CPSC in 1974, there has been almost a decade of debate and delay over these requirements. [19]

Much of the controversy has been stimulated by the widespread use of lawn mowers and the familiarity of the risk. Lawn mowers pose not dimly understood carcinogenic risks but quite apparent and well-known safety hazards. Indeed, nowhere in the CPSC analyses does the agency maintain that there is any market failure whatsoever.

Although markets do not always lead to the optimal product mixture, particularly when there are large fixed costs of different variants of the product and substantial heterogeneity in consumer tastes, these difficulties do not seem compelling in the case of lawn mowers. Any lawn mower company markets a variety of models, which differ in their cutting width, their engine power, and other options, particularly bagging and mulching features, that affect the design of the mower's housing. Unless lawn mower safety is an extremely rare consumer taste, most lawn mower companies have an incentive to introduce a safe model. At the very least, a small, aggressive firm might attempt to establish itself through development of a safe lawn mower.

The market will not generate this outcome if consumers do not view the safety benefits as commensurate with the costs. In the absence of any demonstration of significant market imperfections, the failure of the market to provide a safer lawn mower serves as strong evidence against the regulation's desirability. The calculations below address this issue more explicitly and lead to similar findings.

The position that the CPSC advocates hinges on two main elements: (1) the presence of 77,000 lawn-mower-related injuries annually, 59,000 of which it claims will be prevented by the standard, and (2) benefits of the standard ($211 million annually or, after adjusting for inflation, $262 million annually) greater than the costs ($189 million annually).[20] As in most regulatory analyses, there are numerous assumptions that might arouse some controversy. Rather than engage in an exhaustive critique, I will focus on the fundamental concerns that seem to undermine the desirability of the standard. These concerns have very little overlap with the issues raised by the White House oversight group since I focus on more recent CPSC analyses.[21] Together with the White House comments, they provide a comprehensive critique of the CPSC policy on lawn mowers.

First, even if one takes the CPSC calculations at face value, proper discounting leads to costs in excess of the benefits. The CPSC prepared one cost estimate, $189 million, where the costs are incurred immediately. It also prepared several benefit estimates, so that the benefit-cost performance of the standard is somewhat muddled.

The benefit estimate most prominent in the analysis—and the only estimate appearing in the summary section of the analysis—was $211 million. But this benefit figure is not discounted even though the benefits are spread over an eight-year period. After discounting, the benefit amount drops to $141 million, or $48 million below the costs.[22]

In an apparent effort to bolster the attractiveness of the standard, the CPSC prepared another benefit estimate in which future benefits were adjusted for inflation. In particular, since lawn mower prices had been rising by 6 percent, benefits were also assumed to grow at this rate, yielding total benefits ($170 million) still below costs once the benefits are discounted.[23]

This "inflation adjustment" is somewhat perplexing. It is difficult to find any meaningful link whatsoever between past lawn mower price increases and the future value of preventing lawn mower injuries. If one were to adjust for inflation, all prices should be put in real terms so that only relative price changes would matter. If lawn mower prices are rising in relation to other prices, as the CPSC seems to believe, it is the future *costs* of the standard that are increasing, not the benefits. Upward benefit adjustments should be based on relative changes in consumers' willingness to pay for risk reduction.

Even if we focus on the more reasonable benefit estimates, there is a difficulty about the CPSC's assumptions regarding the standard's effectiveness. The principal provisions of the standard include foot-probe requirements, a "deadman" control system requiring continuous contact with the mower handle, and warning signs. Although the CPSC asserts that these requirements will eliminate 77 percent of all injuries, this figure is speculative.[24] Until the standard is implemented, one can make only a very rough guess about the likely effect, and the CPSC has offered no convincing justification for the 77 percent figure. It could just as well be 1 percent, 40 percent, or 80 percent.

The underlying difficulty is twofold. First, the relation between new lawn mower designs and injuries under different mowing situations is not well understood, especially because we have no experience with the new designs. Second, we do not know how consumers will respond and how their responses will affect safety. Many of the design changes will affect the utility of the mower, which in turn may alter consumers' behavior. The foot-probe guards installed on the 1981 Lawn Boy Supreme, for example, create a minor drag when the lawn mower is moved forward but are a major impediment when it is moved backward, as is necessary when mowing around trees and bushes. After these plastic guards are removed, the rear foot-probe area becomes much greater than if the lawn mower had not been designed to accommodate this protective device.[25] If other consumers do as I did and remove these guards, their lawn mowers will be much more hazardous than the preregulation mower would have been.

Even if we had an accurate assessment of the standard's total effect on safety, such information would not be sufficient. The lawn mower standard is multifaceted, including both foot-probe requirements and an engine cutoff device. A fundamental policy concern is whether these requirements are superfluous. In particular, once lawn mowers are equipped with one of these measures, is the incremental effect on safety of the second measure sufficient to warrant the additional expense?

Although it is possible to speculate on the magnitude of the effects, a more meaningful strategy would be to foster a diversity of approaches rather than mandate uniform design changes for all mowers. A pervasive difficulty with the CPSC approach is that the agency often mounts a multiple attack on a perceived hazard when a more limited approach might be warranted.

Other shortcomings of the CPSC analysis are also of consequence, although their net effect is unclear. By ignoring the increased difficulty of using mowers, particularly from the deadman control device, the CPSC omitted a potentially important loss to consumers. An effect in the other direction is that only financial costs of injuries were counted; the value of pain and suffering, for example, was not included. For most lawn mower injuries, two-thirds of which are minor lacerations, this value may not be great. But for the 10,000 finger and toe amputations, the value to consumers of avoiding the injury will far exceed the medical costs. [26]

What is most telling is that the lawn mower standard cannot be justified on a benefit-cost basis even by using the CPSC's own calculations. Discounting the deferred and overoptimistic benefit projections is alone sufficient to undermine the standard's desirability. Whether or not any components of the standard could be justified on an incremental basis cannot be ascertained from the available data, but some of the regulatory components appear to be redundant. If these were eliminated, the attractiveness of some of the remaining aspects of the standards would be enhanced.

The inadequacies of the CPSC's approach suggest that the prolonged debate over the lawn mower standard may be attributable in part to the failure to make a convincing assessment of the merits of the regulation. By not providing a sound analytic basis for the standard, the CPSC may have contributed to the legitimate criticisms levied against the lawn mower safety effort.

Unvented Gas-fired Space Heaters

The 1980 CPSC analysis of its standard for unvented gas-fired space heaters epitomizes the agency's general approach. [27] After withdrawing a 1979 proposal to ban these heaters, the CPSC focused instead on developing an oxygen depletion sensor system. This detection device was intended to prevent carbon monoxide poisoning from gas-burning heaters. CPSC issued a final rule requiring oxygen depletion safety cutoff systems in 1980, but in 1983 the CPSC proposed a renovation of this standard in favor of compliance with a voluntary industry standard.[28] Here I review the economic merits of this standard, which are not greatly affected by whether the CPSC or an industry group ensures compliance.

It is noteworthy that the commission "instructed the staff to develop a mandatory standard."[29] Although informational alternatives were among the options originally considered by the commission, by focusing the staff analysis on the standards approach the commissioners in effect ruled out other alternatives.[30] Bans and standards are subjected to quite thorough—but not always fully accurate—analyses, but alternatives are not given such extensive treatment. CPSC regulatory analyses consequently follow a classic pattern in which analyses are prepared to justify a predetermined policy rather than letting the results of the analyses guide the policy choice.

The first issue confronted in the regulatory analysis was whether or not the risk was unreasonable. Presumably the reasonableness of the risk hinges on some form of market failure. The CPSC's demonstration of the unreasonableness of the hazard did not go beyond noting that there were seventy carbon monoxide deaths a year associated with unvented gas space heaters.[31]

This estimate was based on extrapolations by the CPSC staff from death certificates, NEISS data, newspaper clippings, and data from the National Center for Health Statistics. Whenever the CPSC projects such low national death rates from a very small sample, the process is fraught with error. Part of this error stems from the small sample; a few isolated deaths do not permit precise inferences about national patterns, as my discussion of the NEISS data indicated. Second, what do the available data mean? Many users of gas space heaters are elderly and have a high mortality rate irrespective of the use of the heaters. The NEISS data are structured to indicate only that a product was *in use at the time of death, not that the product caused the death.* These caveats were never even mentioned in the CPSC analysis, which treated the unreliable and possibly upwardly biased death figures as precise components of the study.

Moreover, the analysis did not mention the annual probability of death to a user of such a heater; nor was the total size of the population of users mentioned in the analysis of unreasonable risk. The annual sales of such heaters, given later in the report, ranged from

120,000 in 1979 to 260,000 in 1966.[32] If the total number of heaters in use is 2.6 million, the annual death risk is quite small, about 3 in 100,000 annually. Whether the heaters should be regulated should hinge on the merits of the regulation, not on an arbitrary determination that the risk is unreasonable. The low risk does, however, suggest that many substitute forms of heaters, such as kerosene or wood-burning stoves (which may cause chimney explosions), may pose even greater risks.

In its assessment of the costs of the regulation, the CPSC dismissed the changeover costs, such as costs of redesign, and ignored any change in the cost of marketing an altered product. The estimated annual cost increase based on the added cost of parts was $5 to $10 per heater. The resulting 5 percent price rise was assumed to have no effect on demand.[33] The CPSC in effect assumes that companies will sell the same number of units at a higher price, including an additional markup. If the assumption were correct, it would be in the companies' financial interest to introduce the modifications without any regulation; since they have not made such changes voluntarily, the assumption is not consistent with observed behavior.

The benefit assessment assumed that the carbon monoxide shut-off device would prevent 90 percent of all heater-related deaths.[34] There was no supporting evidence for this optimistic assumption. When it is compounded with the biases in the assessment of the overall risks to be reduced, the result is a very efficacious standard that saves lives at a cost of $100,000 per life (using an intermediate CPSC cost projection).

Even if these inadequacies were not present, this cost-per-life estimate would be too low because the CPSC is comparing current increases in costs with deferred reductions in deaths. If, for example, the death prevented occurred during the seventh year of the product's life, the cost per life doubles after discounting, to $200,000.

Another difficulty is that the lives saved are those with above-average rates of mortality. The elderly may have a life expectancy of a decade or less, and persons with low incomes, who are likely to buy these heaters, also have shorter longevity. It might be asked: Should extending the lives of these individuals be given the same value as extending the life of a person with a much greater expected longevity? Since safety regulations extend lives only on a probabilistic basis and do not confer immortality, presumably the increased years of life extended matter as well as the number of accidental deaths averted.

A simple adjustment is to calculate the regulation's cost per discounted life-year that is extended. Such straightforward quantity adjustment would introduce much greater comparability among regulations. When carried to its logical conclusion, this approach would create a strong bias in favor of life extension for children, so that the CPSC's emphasis on toy regulations does not seem misplaced.

The quality of the life being extended also matters, and the relation of a quality-adjusted measure of the value of life to age becomes more complex. Parents' investments in child rearing and education of their children presumably raise the value of their children's lives, so that, after discounting appropriately, averting an accidental death for a twelve-year-old may have a greater value than for a one-year-old.

Such refined determinations greatly exceed our existing knowledge of consumers' risk-dollar trade-offs. The purpose of raising these problems is to highlight the complexity of judgments about the value of life so that, even if we begin to calculate costs per discounted life-year extended, we should not be lulled into a false sense of precision. We should, however, attempt to push much closer to a careful analysis of the risk-cost trade-offs than the CPSC has in its past analyses.

More than any other standard considered in this chapter, the standard for unvented gas-fired space heaters may be desirable even after taking into account the length of lives saved, the role of discounting, the efficacy of the standard in savings lives, the imprecision and bias in the underlying risk assessment, and the underestimation of the costs. We cannot be fully confident that this is the case since all these errors are systematically directed at making the standard appear more attractive than it actually is. Moreover, the attractiveness of alternative policies should also be compared with that of the standard, but this cannot be done when the commission confines the economic analysis to a single possibility.

Urea Formaldehyde Foam Insulation

The most prominent recent target for a CPSC ban is urea formaldehyde foam insulation. [35] This insulation is blown into the area between the frame and the outer wall of buildings to retrofit them with greater insulation. As most observers of the advertisements for this product can surmise, it is aimed at consumers who wish to reduce their energy consumption but do not wish to incur the major expense associated with an insulation job of high quality. The undesirable feature of the foam is that it generates formaldehyde gas, which has an unpleasant odor and may also cause cancer and have other adverse effects on health.

The economic analysis prepared by the CPSC is not sufficient to provide a sound basis for proceeding with any formaldehyde ban, although the weakness of the analysis did not deter the CPSC from taking action. The foam insulation analysis illustrates two common failings in its approach—a failure to calculate costs properly and a failure to discount deferred benefits. Other shortcomings, such as the absence of any discussion of inadequacies in the market, are also present, but I will not reiterate these familiar deficiencies.

The only costs included by the CPSC were the forgone energy savings. The costs to producers were assumed to be zero. Since a product ban would lead to a substantial loss of business for many producers and contractors, this assumption is certainly not accurate. Moreover, an imbalance in the CPSC's approach creates a bias toward bans. Whereas costs to producers are calculated for more limited product standards, the neglect of such costs in the case of bans creates a bias against more limited actions. Many costs to consumers, such as the decreased property value of houses now insulated with this foam, are also not included in the overall cost assessment, although they are mentioned by the CPSC. If, however, it was widely believed that the CPSC regulation was misguided, there would be little decline in property values.

The CPSC estimated that the standard would reduce the cancer risk for those exposed to formaldehyde foam by an amount between zero and 0.000086. The CPSC did not rule out the possibility of zero risk. The midpoint of this range is a cancer risk of 1 chance in 25,000. To put this risk in perspective, it is noteworthy that the average American worker faces a fatal job accident risk 2½ times as high every year.[36] The foam insulation risk is certainly not sufficiently large to be a signal of rampant market failure. If the CPSC were basing its policy on the risk level per se, formaldehyde foam insulation would rank below thousands of other policies.

A firm economic basis for CPSC action would be evidence of the cost-effectiveness of this type of risk reduction. Using an intermediate assumption about energy costs (5 percent real growth) and the upper bound on the risk estimate and counting *only* increased energy costs to consumers, we can calculate from the CPSC estimates the discounted cost per cancer case at $148,000. If, instead, we use the midpoint of the assessed risk range rather than the "worst case" approach of the CPSC, the cost per cancer case becomes $296,000. Even this higher estimate does not constitute a clearly unreasonable expenditure to avert cancer.

The difficulty is that, in addition to neglecting many important cost components, the CPSC misassessed the cancer benefits. Although it discounted future energy savings, thus reducing their present value, it did not take into account the deferred nature of the reduction in cancer. The cancer risk estimates were for prolonged

100

exposures of seven years. If we add a gestation period for cancer of at least a decade, the cancer risks averted have a seventeen-year lag, although the increased costs begin immediately. After discounting benefits appropriately, the cost per cancer case jumps to $1.5 million.[37] Longer gestation periods for cancer, which are more plausible, would raise the cost per case even further.

Although the CPSC nevertheless proceeded to ban urea formaldehyde foam insulation in 1982, this action was short-lived. In 1983 the U.S. court of appeals overturned the ban for two reasons. First, the CPSC should have issued the ban under the Federal Hazardous Substances Act rather than under the Consumer Product Safety Act. In addition, the court did not believe that the risk data available were sufficiently reliable. Their unreliability was so great that, as noted above, the CPSC could not rule out the possibility that the product posed zero risk.

Rather than adopt a policy of banning products that pose potentially small risks about which very little is known, the CPSC might be more effective if it addressed its efforts to more consequential targets for government regulations.

In short, the CPSC ban on foam insulation was based on overinflated benefit estimates and understated costs, resulting in a standard that does not appear to be a cost-effective way to avert cancer.

Conclusion

These case studies of CPSC regulatory analyses have shared a number of recurring themes related to both the CPSC's policy approach and the economic merits of its policies. Briefly, they are as follows:

Benefit-cost tests and cost-effectiveness tests are usually omitted, and the regulations would not generally pass such tests if they were performed.

The CPSC does gather some clearly relevant data pertinent to such judgments. This information provided much of the basis for the benefit-cost calculations I have presented. Although the CPSC's legislation does not prohibit such a balanced approach, the CPSC typically falls short of carrying the benefit-cost exercise to its logical conclusion because of the agency's underlying suspicion that such quantification is inappropriate in the light of presumed inadequacies in the ways benefits and costs are measured. Without obtaining reliable estimates of the effects of policies, however, one is forced to rely on a more whimsical approach to balancing the diverse effects. The CPSC's practice of omitting such an explicit calculation of the trade-offs reflects the primary emphasis of its policy making on the risk-related components of the supporting analyses prepared for its actions.

The rationale for intervention is not explicitly considered. There is no discussion of market failures or criteria for determining whether a risk is unreasonable; past policies suggest that any nonzero risk could qualify as unreasonable.

The claim that the CPSC ignores the rationale for government intervention is based specifically on the absence of sound discussion of market failure and how it relates to regulatory policy. The preamble that accompanies proposals and advance notices of proposed rule making usually offers a rationale for the commission's actions, but this rationale is generally in terms of the existence of product-related accidents, which are invariably judged to be "unreasonable." It does not set out an economically sound analysis of market failure. The absolutist approach would be desirable if a no-risk society were optimal, but it has no justification unless all adverse health effects have an infinite value. Such an extreme assumption is inconsistent with individuals' many risk-taking actions and would necessitate allocating the entire federal budget to risk reduction.

The total number of accidents is the focus of the analysis, not the value to society of the likely accident reduction.

Rather than focusing on a use-adjusted accident measure, the commission emphasizes the total number of product-related injuries. It then estimates the incremental reduction in accidents, usually on the basis of very generous assumptions about effectiveness. The major deficiency of this approach is that even if the CPSC's objective is to produce the greatest risk reduction irrespective of cost, it is not following an appropriate strategy. It should focus on the frequency of harm per unit of time that the product is used.

To the extent that the value of benefits is assessed, only financial outlays such as medical costs and forgone earnings are included.

This shortcoming is true of all risk regulation agencies, and in many respects the CPSC may be among the most progressive agencies in this area. The CPSC staff has developed an injury cost model that includes, among other financial costs, the outlays for medical treatment, legal expenses, forgone earnings, and—in a very rudimentary way—pain and suffering. The CPSC should shift its focus from allegedly "economic" measures of accident costs to measures of people's willingness to pay for accident reduction. A good starting point for evaluating these risk-money trade-offs is the value of the wage-risk trade-offs displayed in workers' job choices, which are summarized in chapter 2.

The costs to consumers of having fewer products from which to choose is ignored except where products are modified and remain on the market.

The difficulty is not simply that regulated products will differ from previously available versions in their safety-related attributes. Rather, products subject to extensive regulation or outright bans may disappear from the market altogether. Calculating the loss in welfare to consumers is not always straightforward, but in situations in which the regulation will have a significant effect on what products are available, the omission of such effects from the CPSC's deliberations will create a bias toward overregulation. The CPSC now attempts to capture such concerns by assessing whether there are possible substitutes for highly valued commodities.

The direct costs to firms of product modifications are included, but if a product is banned, the costs to the firm are set at zero. This procedure creates a bias toward fully comprehensive bans rather than selective standards.

The CPSC is required by statute to calculate the effects of product modifications on industry. Although the merits of bans are assessed in a similar manner when product modification is the manufacturer's means of compliance with the ban, the cost calculations are usually not made when a product such as urea formaldehyde foam insulation will no longer be produced. If firms were in fact indifferent to providing this good, as the CPSC assumes, presumably most would not be in that line of business.

Calculations of the risks and the overoptimistic assumptions about risk reduction are based on an accident generation model in which product defects are the driving force and for which CPSC standards are presumed to be effective. Another fundamentally erroneous assumption is that the products and activities that will substitute for the regulated or banned product will impose zero risk. Regulating products imposing an annual death risk of as low as 1 in 25,000, as the CPSC has done, may lead to decreased use of products posing lower risks than those that will take their place.

These shortcomings pertain not only to isolated incidents, such as the flame retardant Tris, which was found to be potentially carcinogenic, but to all products. Whenever the banning or modification of products by CPSC regulations leads to a change in consumption patterns and consumers' activities, the net effect on the riskiness of the consumers' life style must be assessed, not simply the product-specific effect. Coupling an assumption of zero-risk alternatives with very generous assumptions about the efficacy of CPSC regulation creates a very strong proregulation bias.

The role of consumers' safety-related actions and ways to alter them rather than products are largely ignored. Labeling and certification schemes are often dismissed on the grounds that past efforts to warn consumers of a product hazard did not fully eliminate the risk.

Once a hazardous product is identified, the list of policy options seldom includes informational alternatives. More typically, after some preliminary analysis and discussion, a thorough regulatory analysis is prepared for only a single policy mode, such as a ban. The CPSC's bias toward engineering controls may diminish in response to the 1981 amendments to the Consumer Product Safety Act, which bolstered the requirements for mandatory rule making.

Notes

1. For a critique of the original CPSC proposal, see U.S. Council on Wage and Price Stability, *Comments on Proposed Matchbook Standard* (Washington, D.C., 1976), and the companion article by Milton Kafoglis, "Matchbook Safety," in J. Miller and B. Yandle eds., *Benefit-Cost Analyses of Social Regulation* (Washington, D.C.: American Enterprise Institute, 1979).
2. See CFR 1202.
3. See notes 1 and 2.
4. See Council on Wage and Price Stability, *Proposed Matchbook Standard.*
5. See CFR 1202.
6. See note 1.
7. These data are for FY 1980 and appear in U.S. Consumer Product Safety Commission (CPSC), *Annual Report*, pt. 2 (Washington, D.C., 1981).
8. Council on Wage and Price Stability, *Comments on Proposed Matchbook Standard.*
9. My studies of the value of injuries are discussed in chapter 2.
10. For these data see Council on Wage and Price Stability, *Proposed Matchbook Standard;* and CPSC, *Annual Report*, pt. 2 (1981).
11. See CFR 1202.
12. See CFR 1201.
13. This final report was prepared for the CPSC by Gary Stacey and Benjamin Gordon, *Draft Final Report on Analysis of Product Costs and Entry Costs for Architectural Glazing Standards to the Consumer Product Safety Commission*, Battelle Laboratories (1976).
14. Ibid.

15. These assumptions were made in the critique of an earlier CPSC analysis by the Council on Wage and Price Stability, *Comments on Proposed Safety Glass/Architectural Glazing Standard* (Washington, D.C., 1976).

16. This figure in turn should be discounted. My nonfatal accident values are discussed in W. Kip Viscusi, *Risk by Choice: Regulating Health and Safety in the Workplace* (Cambridge, Mass.: Harvard University Press, 1983).

17. Council on Wage and Price Stability, *Architectural Glazing Standard*.

18. See CFR 1205.

19. Past CPSC analyses were the subject of critiques by the Council on Wage and Price Stability, *Comments on Proposed Lawn Mower Standard* (Washington, D.C., 1975 and 1977), and by Thomas Lenard, "Lawnmower Safety," in Miller and Yandle, *Benefit-Cost Analyses of Social Regulation*. My focus is on the subsequent CPSC material by Warren Prunella and William Zamula, "Economic Impact of Blade Contact Requirements for Power Mowers," Consumer Product Safety Commission, internal report, 1979.

20. See Prunella and Zamula, "Economic Impact."

21. See Council on Wage and Price Stability, *Proposed Lawn Mower Standard;* and Lenard, "Lawnmower Safety."

22. See Prunella and Zamula, "Economic Impact," for these diverse estimates.

23. Ibid.

24. Ibid.

25. I made these modifications in my own newly purchased lawn mower after attempting without much success to use the mower with the plastic guards. The modifications consisted of removing several bolts and took only a few minutes. On discussing these modifications with other purchasers of recent lawn mower models, I learned that removal of these guards was not an unusual practice.

26. See CFR 1205 for these data.

27. See the final economic impact report by Roy Sammarco, "Unvented Gas-Fired Space Heaters: Final Economic Impact Report," Consumer Product Safety Commission, internal report, 1980.

28. See 48 FR 45405.

29. Sammarco, "Unvented Gas-Fired Space Heaters."

30. Ibid.

31. Ibid.

32. Ibid.

33. See ibid. for the supporting data cited in this paragraph.

34. Ibid.

35. See Charles Smith, "Urea Formaldehyde Foam Insulation: Preliminary Economic Assessment of a Ban of Sales," Consumer Product Safety Commission, internal report, 1980, for supporting information cited in this paragraph.

36. See Viscusi, *Risk by Choice*.

37. The interest rate used was 10 percent.

7
Policy Proposals

Some critics of the CPSC have called for abolishing the agency or, at the very least, decimating it through increasingly severe budget cuts. The desirability of abandoning this area of government regulation cannot be ruled out a priori. Regulatory agencies share with other economic institutions the property of diminishing returns. Once we have isolated the most promising areas of regulation, the policies will be less desirable as we move further down the list of regulatory targets. The potential efficacy of the CPSC is limited in large part by the exclusion of many of the most important product-related hazards from its jurisdiction—notably, automobiles, airplanes, food, and drugs. The CPSC serves as a catchall safety agency for product risks for which special programs have not been established.

Although the restrictions on the CPSC's authority diminish the total net benefits its regulations can provide, the desirability of its efforts measured in benefits per unit cost imposed could be substantial. Whether these regulatory policies can be effective is quite a different issue from whether they have been desirable in the past. My conclusion is that they have not. Rather than terminate these efforts prematurely, however, it would be preferable to assess the desirability of continuing them after placing them on a more efficient basis. My policy proposals for achieving this reorientation are outlined below.

Abolish the Consumer Product Safety Commission and shift its functions to the executive branch.

The present quasi-judicial structure of the commission is ill suited to addressing the issue of whether there are positive net benefits from regulating a product. Because the major policy choices hinge on economic issues rather than simple interpretations of the law, the commission format is inappropriate. Since the primary objective should be to promote the set of products most desirable to consumers rather than to regulate risks per se, a logical candidate for undertaking this effort is the U.S. Department of Commerce. If meaningful benefit-cost criteria were applied, the policies that emerged would be similar if the CPSC were shifted to an agency such as the Department of Health and Human Services as well.

Shifting these functions to the executive branch is not simply a means of changing the agency's perspective. More important, the administrative checks on the agency's actions would be greatly enhanced. Undertaking product safety regulations within the context of an executive branch agency would make the policies subject to the White House oversight process—a much-needed change. Most important, the CPSC's policies would be based more directly on the overall merits of its efforts rather than on narrowly perceived interpretations of its product safety mission. This centralized review function is also better suited to making comparisons to ensure the cogency of the regulatory analyses and the policies based on them and to making comparisons among agencies to promote individual health most cost-effectively. If the CPSC is not abolished, Congress should extend the authority of the White House oversight process to include independent agencies such as the CPSC. Before President Reagan moved the oversight process to the OMB, the White House oversight group did have the authority to file public comments on rules proposed by independent agencies, although its comments were not binding.

A more ambitious institutional change would be to combine all product safety activities within the Commerce Department, including the FDA, the NHTSA, and the airplane safety functions of the FAA. The argument for specifically targeted regulations is that agencies with mandates related to a specific industry are better able to assess the merits of regulation through their superior knowledge of the industry. The disadvantage is that cross-product comparisons of the desirability of regulations become more difficult once these activities are dispersed. In addition, industry-oriented agencies such as the Department of Transportation may be more likely than an agency with diverse responsibilities to be captured by the industry they regulate. Although there may be a case for the present division of responsibilities, in the absence of a careful weighing of the feasibility of a major restructuring, it is premature to dismiss such a consolidation and the prospects it would offer for more efficient risk regulation.

If such a merger is not undertaken, an enhanced effort should nevertheless be made to promote the most effective set of product safety regulations. If bicycle safety standards save lives at a cost of $5 million per life and safety standards for private planes save lives at $500,000 per life, society's resources could be better spent by loosening bicycle standards and tightening airplane standards.

Eliminate the CPSC's section 15 authority.

Under section 15 of the Consumer Product Safety Act, the CPSC has broad authority to take action against regulated products as well as against products posing substantial risks that are not covered by existing regulations. The wisdom of these actions is not reviewed in a formal rule-making proceeding, and firms have no clear basis for judging what products the CPSC will recall. Since the CPSC now relies almost exclusively on this policy tool, the net effect is the establishment of ad hoc regulatory policy with no built-in checks on abuses except for an appeals process and no regulatory guidelines to enable businesses to make long-run product safety decisions.

By eliminating the section 15 authority, Congress would not be restricting the CPSC to narrow product-specific regulations, although narrowing the scope of the CPSC's approach is not undesirable. The CPSC could retain the benefits of a performance-oriented approach while giving more explicit guidelines to business by promulgating generic standards rather than relying on the section 15 authority. It might, for example, delineate what general types of risks it would address within each class of hazards (for example, flammability). For these risks the CPSC should indicate as specifically as possible on which considerations it would base the subsequent ban or recall decisions.

For such guidelines to be meaningful, the CPSC should ultimately indicate what risk-cost trade-offs it will adopt and what indexes it will use to judge whether the risk is a legitimate hazard that does not merit regulation (for example, baseball) or whether the CPSC will target it for policy action. Finally, when ban or recall actions are undertaken, greater effort should be made to indicate the precedential implications of these actions with respect to related product risks. Although bans and recalls are generally undertaken for defects of specific products rather than for deficiencies of an entire product class, the potential lessons that can be drawn from such actions are often not narrowly defined. By promulgating broadly based rules, the CPSC would be able to provide firmer guidance for businessmen to make product-related decisions while maintaining some of the section 15 flexibility. The rule-making approach would also open up the CPSC regulatory process to public comment and debate, which ideally should enhance the responsiveness of regulatory design to the economic effects of these policies.

Eliminate the "unreasonable risk" criterion and establish an explicit benefit-cost test for all product safety policies.

CPSC policies are currently governed by whether a risk is classified as unreasonable, as apparently all risks are if they can be reduced by CPSC standards or bans. Meaningful definitions of risk focus on use-adjusted probabilities. The CPSC, however, emphasizes the total adverse health outcomes and consequently may regulate frequently used products that are in fact quite safe.

It is not sufficient to alter this approach by regulating only products posing a high risk of adverse outcomes. The need for intervention and whether on balance the policy is desirable must also be assessed. Revising the Consumer Product Safety Act to include an explicit benefit-cost test would ensure that the overall merits of policies were no longer subordinated to their effects on product safety alone.

Unlike the legislation of other risk-regulation agencies, the Consumer Product Safety Act does not impose a criterion for policy design that prohibits a benefit-cost test. In fact, by requiring the CPSC to calculate the critical benefit and cost effects of its policies, this legislation pushes much closer to a benefit-cost requirement than the legislation of other agencies. Unfortunately, since the potential for making sound and balanced regulatory decisions has not been exploited, a benefit-cost requirement may be needed to push the CPSC further in this direction.

The legislative mandate is also important insofar as it affects the criteria to be applied by the White House oversight process, which would gain authority over the CPSC if it were moved to the executive branch. Risk-regulation agencies now subject to this review frequently argue that their legislative mandates require that they ignore such trade-offs and regulate all risks that meet certain tests, such as whether or not they are significant. No similar loophole should be provided to the CPSC if its enabling legislation is revised.

Establish a short-term timetable for the abolition of all current standards and bans, and replace them with an approach that places greater emphasis on safety information and penalties for hazardous products.

The existing standards and bans have been based on a rigid regulatory approach concerned almost exclusively with the existence of a hazard. The primary focus should be on providing the product mix most preferred by consumers. Given the heterogeneity of individuals' tastes and attitudes toward risk, no uniform policy will ever be completely successful in meeting their needs. The informational approach would enable consumers to make the product choices that reflect their attitudes toward risk and also help them select the optimal degree of care in using the product.

If the CPSC can identify major inadequacies in the market that will persist even with increased product safety information, it can consider more explicit regulations. In practice, regulatory efforts directed at providing information may contribute to consumers' confusion since it is unlikely that consumers can make use of risk information about thousands of products. Moreover, the costs of providing the information may outweigh the benefits in improved decisions in some instances, so that regulatory standards (or, equivalently, very severe penalties) will continue to be used. Except in unusual circumstances, regulations should not be enforced through punitive penalties. Penalties should be set at a level to reflect the loss to society from noncompliance. If firms prefer to provide the risky product and pay the penalty and consumers prefer to buy the product despite the higher price resulting from the penalty, they should be free to do so. In many cases in which this penalty approach is viewed as ineffective, it may be that the penalty was not set at the proper level or that the initial policy judgments were incorrect.

Develop product safety data based on use-adjusted probabilities, and expand the role of regulatory analysis in CPSC policy making.

The focus of the data base should shift from the total number of injuries to the frequency of injuries as it reflects the intensity of use of the products. Data on total injuries should consequently be augmented with data on sales of the product, numbers of the product in use, size of the consumer population, and similar information. These data are more appropriate for the prospective benefit-cost analyses required under the third part of my proposal, outlined above.

The prospective policy assessments that are undertaken should be coupled with a much more vigorous assessment of existing policies. The CPSC makes some efforts in this regard; for example, it prepares an annual flammable fabrics report that is required by law. These efforts should be expanded so that particularly effective regulatory strategies can be identified and ineffective policies eliminated.

The overall thrust of these proposals is to increase the use of market forces in dealing with product safety. Greater reliance on an information-oriented approach can best augment market forces to establish incentives for safety while at the same time not eliminating highly valued commodities. The risks posed by different products vary among groups in the population, as do individual attitudes toward risk, and this heterogeneity would be suppressed by resorting to uniform standards and bans.

110

Retaining individual choice is especially important for regulations that do not have uniform benefits for all. The increased use of less flammable fabrics in sofas reduces the risk of death for smokers by decreasing the chance of a fire but may increase the risk to nonsmokers since any fire that does occur will produce more highly toxic gases. Safety caps may raise the risk of poisonings if parents leave the caps off the bottles because they are too difficult to remove or if the caps lead parents to be lax about their children's exposure to hazardous products. Rather than continuing the present narrow and paternalistic approach, policies should reflect the diversity of products available to consumers.

Perhaps most important is to recognize that few of our activities are risk free and that it makes little sense to mount a policy crusade against risks per se. The present myopic concern with risk reduction has led to the banning of products that are perhaps much safer than those that will take their place. Some regulations may lead to the introduction of new hazards, as in the case of the potentially carcinogenic substance Tris, which was used to coat children's sleepwear to comply with the Flammable Fabrics Act.

Even if couched in terms of "unreasonable risks," any policy effort with a risk-based objective will be fundamentally ill conceived. The task for policy is to work with market forces to provide the products that will best enhance consumer welfare.

Bibliography

Akerlof, George. "The Market for 'Lemons': Qualitative Uncertainty and the Market Mechanism." *Quarterly Journal of Economics* 84 (1970), 488–500.

Alpert, Marc, and Howard Raiffa. "A Progress Report on the Training of Probability Assessors." Unpublished manuscript, Harvard University (1969).

Alliance of American Insurers. "Highlights of Large-Loss Product Liability Claims," 1980.

Arnould, R. J., and Henry Grabowski. "Auto Safety Regulation: An Analysis of Market Failure." *Bell Journal of Economics* 12 (1981), 27–48.

Arrow, Kenneth. *Essays in the Theory of Risk-Bearing.* Chicago: Markham Publishers, 1971.

———. "Risk Perception in Psychology and Economics." *Economic Inquiry* 20, no. 1 (1982), 1–9.

Bailey, Martin. *Reducing Risks to Life: Measurement of the Benefits.* Washington, D.C.: American Enterprise Institute, 1980.

Blomquist, Glenn. "Value of Life Saving: Implications of Consumption Activity." *Journal of Political Economy* 87 (1979), 540–58.

Broussalian, V. K. "Risk Measurement and Safety Standards in Consumer Products." In *Household Production and Consumption,* edited by N. Terleckyj. New York: National Bureau of Economic Research, 1976, pp. 491–524.

Brown, Charles. "Equalizing Differences in the Labor Market." *Quarterly Journal of Economics* 44 (1980).

Clarke, Alisone, and William Walton. "The Effect of Safety Packaging on Children's Aspirin Ingestions." Consumer Product Safety Commission, internal report (1978).

Cornell, Nina, Roger Noll, and Barry Weingast. "Safety Regulation." In *Setting National Priorities: The Next Ten Years,* edited by H. Owen and C. Schultze. Washington, D.C.: Brookings Institution, 1976, pp. 457–504.

Crandall, Robert, and Lester Lave, eds. *The Scientific Basis of Health and Safety Regulations.* Washington, D.C.: Brookings Institution, 1981.

Epstein, Richard. *Modern Products Liability Law*. Westport, Conn.: Quorum Books, 1980.

Grabowski, Henry, and John Vernon. "Consumer Product Safety Regulation." *American Economic Review* 67 (1978), 284–89.

———. *The Regulation of Pharmaceuticals*. Washington, D.C.: American Enterprise Institute, 1983.

Hemenway, David. *Industrywide Voluntary Product Standards*. Cambridge, Mass.: Ballinger, 1975.

Insurance Services Office. *Product Liability Closed Claims Survey*. New York: Insurance Services Office, 1977.

Kafoglis, Milton. "Matchbook Safety." In *Benefit-Cost Analyses of Social Regulation*, edited by J. Miller and B. Yandle. Washington, D.C.: American Enterprise Institute, 1979.

Kunreuther, H., et al. *Disaster Insurance Protection: Public Policy Lessons*. New York: John Wiley and Sons, 1978.

Kurtz, Robert. "Review of the Journal Article on the Mattress Flammability Standard." Memorandum to Walter Hobby, Consumer Product Safety Commission, 1981.

Leigh, J. Paul. "Estimates of the Equalizing Difference Curve." *Quarterly Review of Economics and Business*. In press.

Lenard, Thomas. "Lawnmower Safety." In *Benefit-Cost Analyses of Social Regulation*, edited by J. Miller and B. Yandle. Washington, D.C.: American Enterprise Institute, 1979.

Linneman, Peter. "The Effects of Consumer Safety Standards: The 1973 Mattress Flammability Standard." *Journal of Law and Economics* (October 1980), 461–79.

MacAvoy, Paul. *The Regulated Industries and the Economy*. New York: Norton, 1979.

Merrill, Richard. "CPSC Regulation of Cancer Risks in Consumer Products: 1972–1981." *Virginia Law Review* 67 (1971), 1216–375.

National Archives of the United States. *Code of Federal Regulations* 16, part 1,000 to end. Washington, D.C., 1981.

Oi, Walter. "The Economics of Product Safety." *Bell Journal of Economics* 4 (1973), 3–28.

Olson, Craig. "An Analysis of Wage Differentials Received by Workers on Dangerous Jobs." *Journal of Human Resources* 67 (1981).

Oster, Sharon. "The Determinants of Consumer Complaints." *Review of Economics and Statistics* 62 (1980), 603–9.

Peltzman, Sam. "The Effects of Automobile Safety Regulation." *Journal of Political Economy* 83 (1975), 677–725.

Posner, Richard A. *Economic Analysis of Law*. Boston: Little, Brown, 1977.

Prosser, William L. *Law of Torts*. St. Paul: West Publishing Co., 1971.

114

Prunella, Warren, and William Zamula. "Economic Impact of Blade Contact Requirements for Power Mowers." Consumer Product Safety Commission, internal report (1979).

Sammarco, Roy, "Unvented Gas-Fired Space Heaters: Final Economic Impact Report," Consumer Product Safety Commission, internal report (1980).

Shavell, Steven. "Strict Liability vs. Negligence." *Journal of Legal Studies* 9 (1980), 1–25.

Smith, Adam. *The Wealth of Nations*. New York: Modern Library, 1937.

Smith, Charles. "Urea Formaldehyde Foam Insulation: Preliminary Economic Assessment of a Ban of Sales." Consumer Product Safety Commission, internal report (1980).

Smith, Robert S. "Compensating Differentials and Public Policy: A Review." *Industrial and Labor Relations Review* 32 (1979), 339–52.

————. *The Occupational Safety and Health Act*. Washington, D.C.: American Enterprise Institute, 1976.

Spence, Michael. "Consumer Misperceptions, Product Failure, and Producer Liability." *Review of Economic Studies* 44 (1977), 561–72.

————. *Market Signaling*. Cambridge, Mass.: Harvard University Press, 1974.

————. "Monopoly, Quality, and Regulation." *Bell Journal of Economics* 6, no. 2 (1975), 417–29.

Stacey, Gary, and Benjamin Gordon. *Draft Final Report on Analysis of Product Costs and Injury Costs for Architectural Glazing Standards to the Consumer Product Safety Commission*. Battelle Laboratories (1976).

Thaler, Richard, and Sherwin Rosen. "The Value of Saving a Life: Evidence from the Labor Market." In *Household Production and Consumption*, edited by N. Terleckyj. New York: National Bureau of Economic Research, 1976.

U.S. Consumer Product Safety Commission. *Annual Report*, pt. 1. Washington, D.C., 1981.

————. *Annual Report*, pt. 2. Washington, D.C., 1981.

————. *Annual Report*. Washington, D.C., 1982.

————. *Compilation of Laws Administered by CPSC*. Washington, D.C., 1981.

U.S. Council on Wage and Price Stability. *Comments on Proposed Lawn Mower Standard*. Washington, D.C., 1975.

————. *Comments on Proposed Matchbook Standard*. Washington, D.C., 1976.

————. *Comments on Proposed Power Lawn Mower Standard*. Washington, D.C., 1977.

————. *Comments on Proposed Safety Glass/Architectural Glazing Standard*. Washington, D.C., 1976.

U.S. Department of Commerce. *Population Estimates and Projections.* Current Population Reports Series P-25. Washington, D.C., various years.

———. *Statistical Abstract of the United States, 1982–83.* Washington, D.C., 1982.

Viscusi, W. Kip. "An Assessment of the Safety Impacts of Consumer Product Safety Regulation." Center for the Study of Business Regulation, Duke University, Working Paper No. 83-10 (1983).

———. *Employment Hazards: An Investigation of Market Performance.* Cambridge, Mass.: Harvard University Press, 1979.

———. "Frameworks for Analyzing the Effect of Risk and Environmental Regulations on Productivity." *American Economic Review* 73 (1983).

———. *Risk by Choice: Regulating Health and Safety in the Workplace.* Cambridge, Mass.: Harvard University Press, 1983.

Viscusi, W. Kip, and Charles O'Connor. "Adaptive Responses to Job Risk Information." Center for Study of Business Regulation, Duke University, Working Paper No. 83-9 (1983).

A NOTE ON THE BOOK

This book was edited by Gertrude Kaplan and Dana Lane,
of the Publications Staff of the American Enterprise Institute.
The staff also designed the cover and format, with Pat Taylor.
The text was set in Palatino, a typeface designed by Hermann Zapf.
Hendricks-Miller Typographic Company of Washington, D.C.,
set the type, and Thomson-Shore, Inc., of Dexter, Michigan,
printed and bound the book, using Warren's Olde Style paper.

SELECTED AEI PUBLICATIONS

Regulation: The AEI Journal on Government and Society, published bimonthly (one year, $18; two years, $34; single copy, $3.50)

Ethics-in-Government Laws: Are They Too "Ethical"? Alfred S. Neely IV (1984, 58 pp., $4.95)

The Regulation of Pharmaceuticals: Balancing the Benefits and Risks, Henry G. Grabowski and John M. Vernon (1983, 74 pp., $4.95)

The Political Economy of Deregulation: Interest Groups in the Regulatory Process, Roger G. Noll and Bruce M. Owen (1983, 164 pp., cloth $15.95, paper $7.95)

Nuclear Safety: Risks and Regulation, William C. Wood (1983, 89 pp., $4.95)

Meeting Human Needs: Toward a New Public Philosophy, Jack A. Meyer, ed. (1983, 469 pp., cloth $34.95, paper $13.95)

The Regulation of Air Pollutant Emissions from Motor Vehicles, Lawrence J. White (1982, 110 pp., cloth $13.95, paper $4.95)

Federal Coal Leasing Policy: Competition in the Energy Industries, Richard S. Gordon (1981, 44 pages, $3.25)

Prices subject to change without notice.

• *Mail orders for publications to:* AMERICAN ENTERPRISE INSTITUTE, 1150 Seventeenth Street, N.W., Washington, D.C. 20036 • *For postage and handling, add 10 percent of total; minimum charge $2, maximum $10* • *For information on orders, or to expedite service, call toll free 800-424-2873* • *When ordering by International Standard Book Number, please use the AEI prefix—0-8447* • *Prices subject to change without notice* • *Payable in U.S. currency only*

AEI ASSOCIATES PROGRAM

The American Enterprise Institute invites your participation in the competition of ideas through its AEI Associates Program. This program has two objectives: (1) to extend public familiarity with contemporary issues; and (2) to increase research on these issues and disseminate the results to policy makers, the academic community, journalists, and others who help shape public attitudes. The areas studied by AEI include Economic Policy, Education Policy, Energy Policy, Fiscal Policy, Government Regulation, Health Policy, International Programs, Legal Policy, National Defense Studies, Political and Social Processes, and Religion, Philosophy, and Public Policy. For the $49 annual fee, Associates receive

- a subscription to *Memorandum*, the newsletter on all AEI activities
- the AEI publications catalog and all supplements
- a 30 percent discount on all AEI books
- a 40 percent discount for certain seminars on key issues
- subscriptions to two of the following publications: *Public Opinion*, a bimonthly magazine exploring trends and implications of public opinion on social and public policy questions; *Regulation*, a bimonthly journal examining all aspects of government regulation of society; and *AEI Economist*, a monthly newsletter analyzing current economic issues and evaluating future trends (or for all three publications, send an additional $12).

Call 202/862-6446 or write: AMERICAN ENTERPRISE INSTITUTE
1150 Seventeenth Street, N.W., Suite 301, Washington, D.C. 20036